AND
ANOTHER
THING

AND ANOTHER THING

Memories of Family Life with a Psychiatrist

ELIZABETH FENWICK

www.whitecrowbooks.com

Praise for *And Another Thing*

'Elizabeth Fenwick has written a charming and beautifully crafted series of autobiographical vignettes, reflecting with a wry and gentle wit on human foibles in many different family, and social and professional contexts from cricket matches to awkward house guests and law courts proceedings. Her astute observations frequently raise a smile of recognition in the reader and there are many hilarious moments. This is a terrific read – definitely a book to pack for your holidays and even to read aloud to family and friends.'

~ **David Lorimer**, Programme Director of the Scientific and Medical Network. Author, *A Quest for Wisdom: Inspiring Purpose on the Path of Life.*

'Elizabeth captures life experiences in every story with such tenderness and humour that none but the most over-inflated ego could possibly find offence. The volunteers in the Covid vaccination waiting area must have thought me a little strange, laughing out loud as I read these stories to myself. That doesn't happen often. Columns by Alan Coren and Miles Kington sometimes triggered such mirth, and Elizabeth Fenwick is cast in their mould. It's a tribute to Michael O'Donnell and *World Medicine* that they were first published and not suppressed by job's-worth lawyers. And it's high time they reached a wider audience in what must surely become a best-selling book.'

~ **Martin Redfern**, Science writer and former BBC Radio producer

CONTENTS

FOREWORD

When I began to try to put these pieces together in some reasonably logical fashion that might interest a publisher, I realised that there was no truly logical way to describe them. They were all written between 1971, when I was about 35, and 1982, and although I made occasional forays into my childhood and adolescence as well, it certainly couldn't be classed as an autobiography. Was it a Memoire? And what exactly was a memoire anyway? I looked it up on Google. A memoire, Google informed me, is "A collection of memories that an individual writes about moments or events, both public and private, that took place in the subject's/person's life. The assertions made in the work are understood to be factual." That's it exactly, a sort of potted autobiography without the boring bits.

I had always wanted to write, but, until my mid-thirties, I had been occupied either earning a living or caring for small children. I had three of them, was married to a psychiatrist and we were living in South London in the house we still live in 50 years later. *World Medicine*, which described itself as a leisure magazine for doctors, dropped through our letterbox each month. Its Editor was Michael O'Donnell, a doctor who retired from clinical medicine to become a professional writer and, in 1969, became Editor of World Medicine, quickly establishing it as the most entertaining

– and in terms of medical politics – the most irreverent and radical medical magazine.

So, in 1971, just on the off-chance, I sent off to him a piece I had written for my husband's in-house hospital magazine, about the pains and perils of being married to a psychiatrist.

I think that anyone who's a writer would agree that there are few high spots in a life higher than their first acceptance letter from a publisher. A few weeks later I sent them another and that too was accepted. And that for me was the start of ten glorious years when I could write about anything I liked, whenever I liked; though I tried to write a piece each month I was under no compulsion to do so.

At some point during that halcyon decade there was another too-good-to-be-true event. I got a letter from *Reader's Digest* inviting me to lunch and also asking me to write them an article for which they would pay me £600!

£600! Riches beyond my wildest dreams! At the time, World Medicine paid me £100 per piece, a fee which seemed to me to be extraordinarily generous. I went out and bought a new dress for the lunch – it was known in the family ever afterwards as The Editor's Dress. I found it in a trunk a few years ago and tried it on. It was at least three inches too tight all over: puzzling since it was labelled size 14, which is what I take now. Clearly a dastardly plot by clothes manufacturers to lull their customers into a relaxed, celebratory, spendthrift state of mind. Actually, that's exactly the state of mind I was in that day – ever since we'd moved here we'd been wanting to replace the ugly 1930-ish fireplace in the sitting room with something more in keeping with the Victorian house. Our bank account brimming with phantom pound notes, we found a builder, chose a fireplace and had it all done and the room dusted in the time it took me to write an article, send it off and have it rejected by the Digest. I'll always be grateful to them, though. If it weren't for them it would probably have been years and years before we got around to removing that horrible fireplace.

In 1982 Michael resigned from the editorship and shortly afterwards the magazine folded. I carried on writing, worked in publishing, even had a spell as an Agony Aunt in *Cosmopolitan* and on Radio Essex, and wrote books on childcare, adolescence, sexual problems. The fact that my husband is dyslexic and I can spell has been rewarding for both of us. Our collaboration, in which he talks (which he does excellently) and I convert it into the Queen's written English, has produced a series of books on topics I would never otherwise have considered – epilepsy, dreams, past lives, and more recently and age appropriately, on death and dying. Because at 85 we are Old People now, no getting away from it. The little kids who were such a fruitful source of material for me are now themselves the parents of nine adolescent and adult, delightful and endlessly fascinating children.

I must remember to tell those grandchildren to start keeping a diary before it's too late. Memories are the story of one's life, and memories, unfortunately, fade. I never did keep a diary, which is why I was so lucky to be given the chance to help so many of my memories to survive by Michael O'Donnell and *World Medicine*.

It's always been an interesting life but re-reading these memories of that particular period reminds me, gratefully, of how much fun it's been too.

DISCLAIMER!

The characters in these articles bear no resemblance to any of my friends, relatives or acquaintances, living or deceased. The purely imaginary district of Herne Hill, to which I sometimes refer, bears only a passing and coincidental resemblance to the rather seedy South London urban community of the same name. Insofar as the Herne Hill which I occasionally describe is based on anywhere at all (which I deny) I concede that it might possibly be drawn – subconsciously – from the little known hamlet of Smirnoff (pop 25), somewhere on the borders of Turkestan, about which I know nothing and you, I hope, know less.

It is laughable to suggest that any conclusions about my close relatives can be drawn from the bizarre and thoroughly inaccurate descriptions of the husband, children, et al., who appear in these pages. Do I look like the sort of woman who would take the mickey out of her mother-in-law? Finally, I would like to make it quite clear that when I mention my friend Patricia who lives next door, I do not of course mean my friend Patricia who lives next door. To make it even clearer I could, I suppose, always refer to her as Gertrude, but she doesn't look like a Gertrude. She looks like a Patricia and if I started calling her Gertrude it just wouldn't ring true.

I have always had a rather cosy feeling about writing for *World Medicine*, based on the assumption that, give or take a junior registrar or two, you know exactly whom you are talking to. One can sit here (holed up in darkest Smirnoff as the Siberian winter drives against the window panes and the wolves howl outside the door), safe in the knowledge that only a select band of medical persons, capable of signing request cards and adding a legible address, will hear the satisfying thump of WM falling onto the doormat once a fortnight. Of these, perhaps 50 per cent will get as far as tearing the plastic wrapper off with their teeth, and another handful may read the editorial and the last page before putting it on one side to improve their minds – at a later unspecified date. There remain, or so I have always imagined, a small, sympathetic group who actually read it, sifting the grain from the chaff, the warp from the weft, too serious-minded to throw the whole thing into the waste-paper basket, too light-hearted to concentrate only on the informative bits. It used to engender a relaxed, between-these-four-walls sort of atmosphere, knowing that only you and I and my mother were ever going to bother to read anything I wrote.

When someone recently threatened to sue me, I realised this was not so. A variety of people, some of whom are not on the circulation list and not all of whom are well-disposed, get their hands upon it. There is, so far as I know, no black market in once read copies of WM and it is not, or I have never seen it, sold at inflated second-hand prices in the back bookshops in the Charing Cross Road. But it is disquieting to learn that people show it to their friends and that GPs leave it around in their waiting rooms where anyone can pick it up – not as bad as if it were publicly on sale in W H. Smith's or passing through Waterloo Station, but bad enough. I am not unreasonable. I realise that I cannot ask the Editor to take up references on his readers, or to limit the circulation to those who are actually too busy to read it at all, although this would certainly make me feel a lot more secure. And I would not reject out of hand the notion that a discriminating receptionist, casting her eye into the waiting room at 11.15 am and lighting upon some trustworthy patient waiting among the *Mirabelles* and back numbers of the *Daily Telegraph* colour supplements for a 10 am appointment, might slip him a copy of WM in a brown paper wrapper to keep him sweet. Apart from that, do you mind keeping it to yourselves? Just so that I know where I stand.

It is so inhibiting, being sued. The words don't flow like they used to, once one knows they are being examined for malicious intent. So many fascinating stories, which can never be told. One way round it is to resort to the universal disclaimer beloved of Private Eye, although there is not much evidence to show that this really works. There is absolutely no truth, for example, in the rumour I may have mentioned before about Phyllis from the dairy running off with the egg man. It never happened and anyway it's so much water under the bridge and I believe they're very happy now and I'm sure she did the right thing. If she did it. Not that she did.

So, what shall we talk about today? The weather? The fluctuating price of gold? How to make a crème brûlée in the classical tradition of Trinity College, Cambridge? (Never use demerara sugar, whatever the cookery books say. It ruins the flavour.) Forgive me if I don't touch on anything more personal for a while. I had it in mind to tell you the story of my aunt and her young man who wore real silk underpants, but I'll give that one a rain check. Not that I think my aunt would make trouble within the family but let us not take any unnecessary risks. Besides, I am very fond of my aunt, and if you think otherwise, you are as nutty as a fruitcake. Sorry, I take that back.

Dear me, how quickly paranoia sets in. I used to think it was all right if it was true, but apparently truthful revelations stimulate more wild indignation than flagrant lies. Truth is beauty and beauty is only skin deep; scratch around there and you can uncover some pretty sensitive spots. Moreover, it takes less effort to throw a brick than toss a bouquet; anger gets the adrenalin flowing more effectively than joy. Fenwick's first law of human nature states that out of every ten people moved to pick up a pen and comment on something they have read, five are seizing a convenient platform for their own irrelevant views, four are offensive, three reproachful, two friendly and one wants to sue.

How does anybody manage to write anything without a perpetual image of his subject matter behind him, idly tossing a writ from hard to hand, wondering whether to lob it into court? Sometimes I'm asked if I've ever thought of writing a novel (who hasn't?). Plenty of characters, I always say, no plots. Now I know I can't even use the characters. It's easy to see why people say we've all got one book in us – it's the one with ourselves dead centre and our nearest and dearest playing supporting roles. Once that's out of the way, once you have to rely on the outside world or your own fevered imagination, you're in trouble.

Did Dickens have this problem? Did Tolstoy? Dostoevsky? Art, after all, is meant to mirror life. And if you see Art, tell him I don't mean him.

This one had a happy ending – a diplomatic intervention by the Editor, and a telephone call between me and the complainant resulted in no lawsuit and no hard feelings. But it did teach me a basic lesson in journalism – never assume that no one actually reads anything you write.

IN THE BEGINNING

1

Get out the flags

~

Empire Day has come and gone once again. It was a great relief to be able to sit back and let it pass me by. Not that it's called Empire Day anymore – it's called Commonwealth Day and has to share the Queen's official birthday with her. But when I was at primary school it was Empire Day still and merited a day of its own, May 24, and we celebrated it in a style the memory of which even now brings a blush to my cheeks and causes my toes to curl inwards inside my shoes.

Of course, it was always hot on May 24. You remember the way it used to be hot in May and June and July and August as well? Little girls used to wear summer dresses with puffed sleeves and short white socks, and panama hats with the elastic always a bit too tight beneath our chins. We would saunter to school in the sunshine with our blazers over our arms, because it was too hot to wear them and

1

anyway, being utility standard and unlined, they tickled so much that we were reluctant to put them on.

We would know, once we got to school on May 23, that Empire Day was imminent, nay, inevitable, because Miss Washington would get out the flags. Miss Washington was our headmistress. Actually, she was our only mistress. She sat us in rows, the youngest at the front and the oldest at the back, and she taught all things to all ages, including tables and chain stitch and how to make paper lanterns at Christmas time and a language she asserted was French, although my parents had grave doubts about it. Nothing I learnt at Miss Washington's school have I ever forgotten, except how to do chain stitch, and that is a great deal more than I can say for later, greater academic institutions, which have had me in their thrall. Even things that I have tried rather hard to obliterate from memory, like the words of the song we used to have to sing on Empire Day, remain etched there with awful clarity.

Miss Washington was short and stout and looked more like a frog than anyone I have ever seen before or since. She worshipped three deities, God, the King and Winston Churchill, and I would not care to guess at the order in which she ranked them. Of the three, Churchill was the only one whose picture hung on the classroom wall and she talked about him more reverently and more often than about God, or even the King. Besides being our headmistress she was an alderman and a Conservative, with a fervour that seemed at least as much religious as political. At eleven o'clock each day she would make herself a cup of tea, placing two Marie biscuits in the saucer and carrying it over to her desk and the tea would slop over the edge of the cup, soaking the ends of the Marie biscuits. She would drink the tea with a slurping sound, dunking the rest of the biscuit. In my memory, crumbs of damp Marie biscuit cling forever around her mouth.

The only subject Miss Washington did not teach us herself was dancing. For this, outside help was brought in twice a week and the girls learned to dance the Skater's Waltz, wearing muffs. We all learned ballroom dancing, too, which caused regular widespread heartbreak because all the girls wanted to dance with Peter Spencer and none of us wanted to dance with Harry Mason or Ronnie Wills. Peter Spencer always used to choose a girl called Brenda Martin to dance with and the rest of us had to wait for the progressive barn dance to get a look in. Brenda Martin was a giggly girl who had a mauve, satin, smocked dress for parties that I thought was beautiful.

Some years ago I met her again; she's a plain woman with an irritating laugh and a perfectly dreadful husband and I couldn't help feeling pleased at life's way of sometimes redressing the balance.

Miss Washington taught us three hymns, which we sang in rotation throughout the term: "Oh God Our Help in Ages Past", "Eternal Father Strong to Save" and "Jerusalem". It never struck me as odd that we should sing once or twice a week for those in peril on the sea, miles though we were from the nearest stretch of coast, which was Blackpool, but I did have some confused thoughts about Jerusalem, feeling sensitively that it was rude of Blake to refer to the cotton mills surrounding us as dark and satanic.

But on Empire Day our singing took a more patriotic turn. We sang "God Save the King" (all three verses) and "Land of Hope and Glory" and "The Soldiers of the Queen"; The Queen, not the King. Not just because Miss Washington's imperialism was rooted in the nineteenth century, though it undoubtedly was, or that she was a woman liberated ahead of her time, although she might have been, but because the rhyme scheme of the song demanded a female sovereign ("We're the soldiers of the queen, my lads, who've been, my lads and seen, my lads . . ." and so on and so, appallingly, forth.) We sang these songs marching up and down our playground carrying flags and there were enough flags for us all, even the smallest children. Such a brave show as we must have made was almost bound to attract attention

3

and indeed it did. We assembled in the brilliant May 24 sunshine, sorting out our flags and being arranged by Miss Washington in strict height order so that I, always gawky, could not even achieve a degree of anonymity among the girls but had to march between Harry Mason and Ronnie Wills. Instantly, as if by magic, an audience materialised.

The audience was between two and ten years old. It lolled over the low playground wall, which should have had iron railings protectively along it, only they'd been requisitioned to make tanks with. It looked grubby, neglected, and most of it should undoubtedly have been at school itself. It was confident, vocal, insolent, and infinitely superior to us. One could not, for the moment, have imagined higher bliss than being Them and not Us, in not having to wave a flag, not having to mumble the unbelievably embarrassing words of "The Soldiers of the Queen", eyes cast down, glued to the back of Ronnie Wills' wrinkled grey woollen socks. "Chin up, Elizabeth. Sing out," cried Miss Washington, for whom personal pride was as nothing compared to national pride. Occasionally she would make sudden rushes at the intruders on the wall, sometimes dislodging a few with her flag, but they were half-hearted attempts, doomed to failure. In any case, I think she rather enjoyed adversity, perhaps realising that Empire Days were numbered and gaining some moral satisfaction in maintaining standards and ceremonials in a changing, unappreciative world. "Take no notice," she would say when the jeers and heckling threatened to overwhelm us. This might have been possible for her – as one of the only two Tory councillors in a northeast Lancashire town known locally as Little Moscow, she was used to opposition and blossomed under it, but we were cast in a different, flabbier mould. "And we'll fight for England's glory, lads", we sang unhappily, ready, to a child, to turn and run should the watchers on the wall show the least sign of translating words into actions.

I never had to wave any more flags after I left Miss Washington's and I wasn't a bit sorry. My next school felt more strongly about the kingdom hereafter than the empire here, and our main May festivity was Ascension Day, which we used to celebrate more enjoyably, if less appropriately, by taking a trip to the Shakespeare Memorial Theatre at Stratford-on-Avon. But looking back on it all now, I am amazed to be overcome by a slight feeling of nostalgia. I can't think why. Not for Miss Washington, putting her flags away in the dusty cupboard for another year. Not even for the fact that our children will have no occasions more picturesque than Referendum Day or the birthday of Charles de Gaulle to wave their flags for. Not, surely not, for the Soldiers of the Queen, marching up and down their playground with the tarmac bubbling in the heat. I suppose it can only be for the weather.

2

Party Time

~

Amazingly enough, for on paper it had nothing going for it at all, my school Centenary Dance (for Prefects and Sixth Formers only) was the first party I really enjoyed. I'm not counting earlier parties with my junior school friends, where we all sat on the floor and played Kim's game and had treasure hunts and watched Mickey Mouse silent 8mm films. Those were fun and the reason they were fun was that there were no boys, or rather there were boys, but only boys like Harry Mason and Ronnie Mills. They didn't count as boys because one saw them every day and played rounders with them and knew that Ronnie Mills still sometimes wet his pants, which gave one a built-in advantage and meant that the question of shyness was irrelevant. But all other parties, at any rate until the Sixth Form and Prefects' Centenary Dance, were purgatory, because I was shy, which meant I was frightened of boys because one is very seldom shy with one's own sex. With the drippiest, dullest, least attractive woman one can always talk about Sainsbury's or how advanced her children are, whereas with a drippy, dull, unattractive man there is nothing to be done but go away and hope to find one more attractive and considerably less dull and drippy.

It must have been boys en masse which precipitated the shyness syndrome, because boys individually were always desirable, romantic love-objects. Naturally one looks for a traumatising formative experience. On my fifth birthday I wanted to ask a little boy with brown eyes in my class to my party, although I didn't know his name. I just mentioned it casually to my mother and there at my party he was, and I was very impressed that my mother had wrought this miracle. But something must have happened at that party, because I can remember hiding in the air-raid shelter while two bigger, more confident girls tried to persuade me to come out. "Come out," they said, "do come out. It's all right now." I wish I could remember what had driven me in but I'm fairly sure it wasn't the little boy with brown eyes.

There's another memory from about the same era, which has a lot to answer for. My mother leading me, a snivelling 5-year-old, away from somebody's front door and saying desperately, "But if you keep on wanting to go home, people just won't ask you to their parties anymore." I couldn't believe that anything so marvellous could actually happen but it seemed to me a utopia worth striving for. The hostess at that party was a splendid woman, rather like the Ark Royal, and she had taken me by the hand and attempted to integrate me into the centre of the room, where a morass of grey-flannel suited boys - much, much bigger and older than me, about 6, were rolling on the floor punching each other in a tangle of short trousers and bare knees. It must have been just about then I started screaming for my mother. I suppose there were other girls at that party, too, but I don't remember any. It seemed to be just me and Them, and if I had been brave enough to stick it out we might have found common ground in hunting a thimble together and avoided the troubled years, which lay ahead.

The Ark Royal's parties terrorised the rest of my childhood and early adolescence. It is enormously unfair to her that they should have done, because she was the kindest possible woman, hell-bent on giving everyone the nicest possible time. She cruised about the room allowing no shirking, lurking, or cringing in corners. She had an inexhaustible stock of games demanding forfeits and variations on charades and, with her own boundless depths of self-confidence, had no patience with anyone else's reluctance to join in. Because shyness is the most selfish, inward-looking emotion, I thought these parties were my own personal misery, directed at me alone. Then, years afterwards, talking to one of those same brawling, short-trousered little boys, he told me he'd been as terrified of them as I was, sick with nervousness for hours beforehand. Self-consciousness makes cowards of us all.

Later on there were Pony Club dances, NSPCC dances, RSPCA dances. The little boys had grown up very nicely with lovely manners and dinner jackets, and now the terror that they might notice you and ask you to dance was matched by the terror that they mightn't. It was awful if nobody fancied you, and shrivellingly embarrassing if they did, unless it was the one you secretly fancied yourself, but it never was.

These dances were mostly held at the Regency Ballroom in Nelson, where the ceremonies were mastered by a couple called Freda and Norbury. Freda was very Come Dancing, Ice Queen of the Tango, swathed in myriad layers of tulle, amazingly lint-white hair tortuously curled on top of her head. The glacial smile chiselled on her features was only ever seen to falter when Norbury, altogether a more human character, removed his wig at the end of the Gay Gordons to mop the sweat off his domed, bald head with the tails of his coat. Wild rumours circulated about Freda: that beneath all the tulle and Elizabeth Arden she was 50, 60, 70, 80 if she was a day; that she had her hair done every Thursday and thereafter never touched it, sleeping every night but Wednesday on a Chinese wooden pillow. Hard on Norbury, we thought.

9

With all this conditioning behind me, no wonder the thought of the Prefects' Centenary Dance struck terror to my marrow. Partners were imported from the local boys' school. We entered the library from one end, the boys from the other, and, in the middle, by the librarian's desk, our headmistress stood like Noah, pairing us off as we came in.

It was of necessity a very proper affair: the staff, matronly vigilantes, sitting around the walls, the school porter patrolling the grounds. Afterwards a girl called Batty Riley claimed that she had been discovered in the bushes by the porter, but only the very gullible believed her. For one thing, there was no bush big enough to conceal even the smallest misdemeanour; for another, you had only to look at Batty Riley.

Of course, the idea was that after the first official coupling, we would all circulate and mix and introduce our partners to each other. Naturally, there was never a hope of that. Anyone lucky enough to have drawn someone even halfway presentable hung shamelessly onto him, avoiding the wildly signalling eyes of friends partnered by 5-foot acne-sprinkled weeds. The rest touted their partners around like second-hand car dealers trying to dispose of an inferior model and eventually ended up eating jellies in the gym, leaning disconsolately up against the parallel bars.

I rather liked my partner. I have no idea whether he liked me. That was absolutely immaterial. The point was that I knew perfectly well that if I played my customary, shy, gawping, silent role, Jennifer Skinner would have him off me in a flash. I worked as hard that night as I've ever worked on any sexual relationship, before or since, and it lasted the night, which was all I wanted of it. It was also the beginning of the end, though of course there were relapses, for the shyness. Quite soon after that I went up to Cambridge and there, with a male/female ratio of 10:1, the cure was more or less completed, by a process known in the psychiatric trade as flooding.

3

How I became a medical student
without really trying

It would be nice to think that it was the usual combination of laudable motives which drew me towards the medical profession, but it wasn't altogether like that. Partly it was the fault of an uncle who, when I was ten or so, gave me a microscope, together with a box of slides of esoteric though only marginally biological interest: sections of pigeons' tongues, bats' eyelashes, larks' spurs, that sort of thing; straight from some witch's kitchen. He was a biology master at a respectable public school. I can't think where he got them. He compounded this by handing over a very fine set of dissecting instruments, and these I carried about hopefully for some years, waiting for one of the family pets to die. Desperate for a specimen, I devised an ingenious method for gassing earthworms, but my mother put a stop to it on the grounds of safety, and even I felt that it lacked humanity. They don't gas easily, earthworms.

All might have been well had I not, the summer I was 14, found a fox, dead in a ditch. We were staying in Southern Ireland at the time. It was warm and humid, semi-tropical down there; palms and possibly mangroves flourished in the hotel grounds. I lugged the carcass back by its tail and showed it to the rest of the family as they were about to go into lunch, but their own curiosity in nature's wonders seemed dormant. However, somebody gave me the use of a small workbench in a garage and there I spent the ensuing days, happily unravelling systems with my new forceps and scalpel. I was regarded as something of a novelty by the other hotel guests, and at first I had a gratifying stream of visitors, handkerchiefs to noses, calling in for an uninformed but enthusiastic demonstration. But, as the holiday wore on, the days grew hotter and the fox grew higher, everyone else's interest suddenly dropped off and it was with some reluctance, and mostly because I felt I had a reputation to keep up, that I set off for the garage each morning. "She wants to be a doctor," my parents explained proudly to the rest of the guests. Well, that's what I thought at the time, but now I'm not at all sure it was proudly that they said it; probably it was defensively, or apologetically. After all, how would I feel if an adolescent daughter of mine shut herself up all summer in an outhouse with a decaying fox? Eventually somebody must have felt sorry for me, because the corpse had vanished one morning and I took no steps to find it.

I'm not at all sure that I did want to be a doctor, even then. It was probably something I dreamed up on impulse to account to the Irish for my bizarre behaviour, but you know how it is when these ideas get put about. The trouble with praiseworthy ambitions is that people fall over themselves to help you to achieve them. I had a suspicion that I wasn't really serious about it myself when, a couple of years later, I deliberately bought a wristwatch without a second hand, so that I couldn't take people's pulses, but everyone else was so keen that it hardly mattered. After a couple of terms in the science sixth, though, I recognised a real snag: I hated science. But medicine isn't science, I told myself, firmly; medicine is people and the rest is but a stepping-stone. "You can go to Cambridge and read Natural Sciences," they said, and although I wasn't sure about the science I liked the idea of Cambridge. Joan Bakewell described somewhere recently her awe, on going up to Cambridge, of the "sophisticated girls from public schools". Now, when I went up for my Cambridge interviews, wearing my nice public school green uniform and my prefect's badge, I met girls who hadn't been to public schools who were wearing *lipstick* and talking about *men*, and they seemed to me to be approximately 100 per cent more sophisticated than the Champs Elysée. I tell you, Joan Bakewell, there are times when a prefect's badge is no comfort at all. In the face of this sort of competition is it any wonder that I hesitated to tell anyone that I didn't think I *was* a natural scientist, and I didn't hold out too much hope of becoming a man-made one either?

But even then I could have taken avoiding action, like a friend who, on our first exploratory foray to the anatomy schools, wandered into the dissecting room under the impression that it was some sort of canteen. She cycled straight back to Girton and told her tutor she wanted to change to moral sciences, but I didn't have that sort of courage. Anyway, it wasn't that I was squeamish, just totally lacking in curiosity. In fact the dissecting room was fun in an earthy sort of way. Its major-domo was a lugubrious fellow called Ron, whose constant companion, as he wandered round the room picking up the bits, was a large Alsatian dog, which makes me think a bit now, although it didn't then. Ron didn't much care for medical students, but he liked girls, and, as a mark of his especial favour, he would take you into the cold storage room and show you next term's corpses, hanging in rows, suspended by their ears.

No, the trouble was science again. The place was rife with it. Organic chemistry was science, with suave Dr Saunders who had two lab assistants brushing him down before he made his entrance, and two jokes in each lecture, nicely spaced. I didn't like organic chemistry. I didn't much like physiology either, although I'd expected that at least to be medicine and not science. In my final practical exam I was reduced to something very like cheating. As we filed into the laboratory we each drew a numbered ticket from the sadist on the door, indicating which set of apparatus was ours to while away the next three hours. It was a kind of Russian roulette as far as I was concerned, but I had made a clandestine arrangement with a friend that, should I draw anything involving electrical circuitry and he not, we should swop. Any guilt I felt was outweighed by the sight of my neighbour, a girl who felt about science much as I did, holding two spare ends of wire and weeping quietly into her rheostat.

I hated biochemistry. It was the Age of Discovery in the Cambridge biochemistry department at that time, with Nobels sprouting like mushrooms at dawn, which was all very nice for them, but hard on us. Textbooks were out of date before the print had dried on them, so we had to go to lectures to get it all from the horse's mouth. Even so, several times a term our lecturers would bound in, scarlet with the manic flush of fresh achievement and we would all resignedly flip back the pages and strike out last week's notes. I quite liked pathology, mostly because of Professor "Daddy" Dean, who was 80-odd and most upset by the whole idea of lady medical students. He did what he could to preserve our innocence by refusing to let us attend the lectures on venereal diseases. Instead, we were told to spend the morning in the library, where he had thoughtfully laid out the relevant textbooks, open at the appropriate pages, so that we could absorb it all without being subjected to coarse male gibes. I daresay there's a whole generation of Cambridge-trained women doctors who aren't too confident when faced with a gonococcus or a spirochaete.

It has always been a matter of some irritation to me that my husband approaches examinations with as much equanimity and as little apparent preparation as he approaches breakfast. You could say that this is a sign of a superior intellect, but I don't like to look at it that way. I think it is something to do with hormones, but I haven't quite worked out what. At any rate, the even tenor of life in the men's colleges always seemed unruffled by the advent of exams, while Girton took on the air of a women's mental hospital wing under siege. We refused invitations and barricaded ourselves in with giant-sized tins of Nescafé; svelte girls who would not normally be seen dead in Hall turned up for dinner unwashed, unbrushed, unkempt; neuroses waxed and proliferated under mutually perpetuated panic.

Altogether, it was with something like relief that I discovered I had only got a third in Anatomy in my final exam, instead of the second necessary for 2nd MB exemption. It seemed like a good natural end point to my medical career. There were several of us making fearful, heart-searching decisions at this time, along the same lines. There was our friend Anthony, who's now a chartered surveyor, and liking it, and a chap whose real name I can't remember but who, for some reason that now escapes me, we called Synchronous Flywheels. He took it hard, Synchronous. We were all sitting in somebody's rooms, I remember, with those who were OK comforting those who weren't, and managing to generate quite a cheerful atmosphere, when old Synchronous came in and spoilt it all. "I'm a failure, oh God, I'm a failure," he kept muttering and the rest of us kept saying, "Oh shut up, Synchronous, of course you're not a failure." I think he became a drug rep, after a spell selling encyclopaedias, and he's probably just as happy as I am.

I do feel a twinge of regret every now and then, but mostly when I see friends in family planning clinics making bombs out of coils. If the twinges get too severe I just take a walk around the hospital. When I see all those nice young doctors, carrying their piles of computer output, going on double-blinds, worrying about the statistical significance of their patients, I know how right I was. Medicine is Science and I'm well out of it all.

4

From the desk of the personal assistant

⌒

In the days when I was kicking around waiting to get married, one of the things I did to pass the time was to work for a branch of the J. Arthur Rank Organisation. Probably by now it has withered and died or been sloughed off as unprofitable; but then it had only recently been taken over and J. Arthur and his organisation were in the process of upgrading it from a sleepy old Midlands family firm to a whizz-bang streamlined modern affair.

For purposes of anonymity, I'll call the firm Bailey, Bailey & Hogsbaum, although Messrs Bailey and Bailey and Hogsbaum were long since dead and had been replaced by Mr Stoke (managing director), Mr Trent (research director) and Mr Wylie-Jenkins (sales director). At the time of the takeover J. Arthur, in the persona of John Davis (who was then only on his second or third wife but showing signs of early ruthlessness), appointed over the heads of this lot a whizz-bang, streamlined, modern chief executive called Algie Lucas. This was common practice in takeovers but did not always make for harmonious relationships. Messrs Stoke and Trent stayed glowering in their Midlands offices, behind the new chief executive in the letter but not the spirit. But Mr Wylie-Jenkins, who had been a pilot officer during the war and fancied himself as a bit of a lad, was quite glad of the opportunity to spend part of the week based on the new London office, where he rolled in at ten, took three-hour lunches and, so the slander had it, spent his evenings in a flat full of dancing girls.

Algie Lucas himself had two personal assistants: one to take round with him everywhere – a very, very efficient lady called Una Jolsson – and one to keep in London, who was me. Because I was called a personal assistant and not a secretary it was understood that I would sometimes have difficulty reading back my shorthand. I had also to undertake various other personally assisting duties such as fetching Algie his car from inaccessible corners of multi-storey carparks and sometimes, if Una Jolsson was not available, driving him up to the Midlands factory in it. He would have preferred to drive it himself, dictating memoranda to me the while and thus saving time in a streamlined, modern way, but taking dictation in the car made me sick so he had to let me drive and write his own notes.

Bailey, Bailey & Hogsbaum made very accurate machine tools. There was the Bailey-Rond, which made things perfectly round and the Bailey-Flat, which made them perfectly level and the Bailey-Silk, which made them perfectly smooth. The zenith of their achievement, the machine which occupied pride of place in all their advertising literature, was the Bailey-Hoo, which could engrave the Lord's prayer on the head of a pin. At machine tool exhibitions the Bailey-Hoo was placed on a small central dais, the pin beside it under a microscope, a salesman standing protectively by, like the keeper of a rare, delicate animal, ready to adjust the microscope for the unbelieving customer so that the prayer sprang into sudden, indisputable clarity. "But what is it for?" I would sometimes ask, "What does it do?" "Do?" they would cry indignantly. "What does it do? Why, this machine is so precise, so accurate, so finely adjusted, that it can write the Lord's Prayer on the head of a pin."

Within the company all the machines were known by their initials and so were all the employees of sales or executive rank, so that internal memos and minutes of executive meetings read as though they were in code. Sometimes I would have to take the minutes of these meetings, which were almost entirely concerned with estimating the prices and possible production dates of new models of the BR and the BF and the BS and the BH and explaining why earlier models had failed to meet their production dates and exceeded their costs. The word they bandied freely across the table in these discussions was "guesstimate", which used to irritate me because I didn't believe there was any such word and, if there was, that it could mean any more than guess or less than estimate. Every time anyone used it I would write down "estimate" firmly, and when Algie Lucas went through the minutes and wrote down what everybody had really said, he would strike out estimate and substitute guesstimate. It was just one of the unwritten rules in the business game. For some reason, if you said your estimate was a guesstimate, then nobody was entitled to complain when it was nine months or £900 out, which it always was.

The export manager was a man known behind his back as the Japanese Admiral, because of a self-important strut and ruddy features, but his real name was Eric. The admiral was directly responsible to the sales director, Charles Wylie-Jenkins, whom he hated because he thought, quite rightly, that while he, Eric, was slaving away dashing around the continent getting orders, CW-J was sitting with his feet on his desk doing damn all and getting all the credit. In fact, Eric loved his job and was especially proud of the way he was building up trade with the East Bloc countries. He was always going off for trade exhibitions in places with no vowels to speak of, like Brno or Przemysl, and getting postcards in languages we couldn't even identify, signed Olga. The London office manager used to pretend to be able to read these and hand them over to him with knowing looks and he'd snatch them away and stuff them into his briefcase looking even redder than usual. He put a lot of effort, not very successfully, into establishing friendly relations with the Russian Trade Delegation up in Highgate, and once organised a little party for them in the office. We all helped him to buy nuts and crisps and plenty of drink to loosen them up, but they were a surly, mistrustful lot who never left each others' sides all evening and were obviously under standing orders not to raise their blood alcohol levels by so much as a milligram.

One day Eric came into the office in a state of extreme agitation. Something really dreadful had happened, he told us. A business friend of his, Greville Wynn, had been arrested by the Russians as a spy. Naturally it was all a ghastly mistake but it was up to him, Eric, to ring up the appropriate authorities and put it right. As good as his word, Eric spent the whole day on the telephone pleading with the Foreign Office, consulates, ambassadors, even the surly fellows up at Highgate, and explaining to them all that Greville was a perfectly ordinary businessman: an honest, simple chap who wouldn't know how to con the recipe for butterscotch sauce out of his grandmother. But nobody seemed interested. Disheartened, disillusioned, he sat at his desk with his head in his hands and we all tried to comfort him. "But it can't be true," he said in honest bewilderment. "I never knew a thing about it." "Well, you wouldn't, would you, Eric," we said reasonably. "I mean, he wouldn't say to you, 'Hang on a minute, Eric old chap, you wait for me at the bar and hold these microdots while I just go and worm a few secrets out of that KGB man over there." For days he kept shaking his head and muttering, "Greville, of all people, Greville. I'd never have believed it." I suppose he was probably jealous, feeling that if MI5 had really wanted a good man with contacts and influence behind the iron curtain they'd have done a lot better to get in touch with him. But at the time he seemed to take the whole affair so personally that I wondered whether he might somehow have got himself mildly involved in the espionage business. Whether perhaps in a moment's undisciplined revelry with Olga he had let slip the secret of the Bailey-Hoo machine and was afraid that even then, in a basement beneath the Kremlin, teams of Russian technicians were working day and night scratching Das Kapital in small Cyrillic characters upon a pinhead.

Now, to the casual observer, things in Bailey, Bailey & Hogsbaum chugged along in pretty much the same way as the months rolled by. Messrs Stoke and Trent sniping at the chief executive with small arms behind his back; the chief executive complaining about the old-fashioned methods and attitudes of Messrs Stoke and Trent; the Japanese Admiral rushing hither and yon with a suitcase and a couple of drip-dry shirts and Mr Wylie-Jenkins putting in an occasional appearance at the office when he knew the Japanese Admiral was out of the country and therefore couldn't buttonhole him about the possibilities of opening up trade in Tibet. In the distance, mortar fire and cymbals clashing could occasionally be heard from Rank headquarters in South Street but, like bombs in Belfast, these occasions, although theoretically troubling, were not close enough to home for personal discomfort.

But, one Monday morning, I arrived in the office to find Algie Lucas packing his bags. At 5.30 the previous Friday when I'd gone home he'd been chief executive of Bailey, Bailey & Hogsbaum; half an hour later he'd been relieved of his post. The grounds for dismissal concerned a letter to an American associate company with whom there had been some dispute and it was possibly a peremptory letter, possibly a tactless one but, Una Jolsson assured me bitterly, what was quite certain was that Messrs Stoke and Trent had helped him, urged him, egged him on to write it, knowing full well what the consequences would be.

I had a look at the letter and it didn't look like a sacking offence to me. I thought of the loyalty a hospital doctor

And Another Thing

expects, and gets, from his superiors when mistakes are
made, when things go wrong and there are lives at stake.
And at least, when the long knives start flashing, there's
recourse to the MDU. Pity the poor business executive. It's
an odd business where the loyalties are only expected to
flow one way.

*Greville Maynard Wynne (1919 – 1990) was a British engineer
and businessman. He was recruited by MI6 because of his frequent
travel to Eastern Europe and acted as a courier to transport top-
secret information to London from Soviet agent Oleg Penkovsky.
They were both arrested by the KGB in October 1962 and convicted
of espionage. Penkovsky was executed and Wynne sentenced to
eight years at Lubyanka Prison. He was released in 1964, in
exchange for a Soviet spy.*

5

Not a word to Chapman Pincher*

~

Michael O'Donnell's memories of military security (World Medicine, November 29), reminded me, somehow, of the time my colleague Dave Harwood and I moved the classified section of the Medical Research Council Registry from Old Queen Street to Park Crescent back in 1961.

I can't remember now why the mantle of such grave national responsibility fell upon our shoulders. I suspect it was because while we were considered senior enough to be trusted with the State's secrets, we were still junior enough to be dragooned into giving up our Saturday morning to take care of them. Actually, I didn't mind at all. There was an air of heady excitement about the job, which was more exciting than the everyday routine of drafting correspondence for the MO who would redraft it in his own style for the SMO, who would redraft it in *his* own style for PMO's approval, who would alter one or two finer points and send it back down the line again for SMO's signature. Sometimes, if the day took me that way, I would self-effacingly produce my draft in the style of the MO, who might, spurred on by my example, redraft it in the SMO's style. Either way, the system kept a lot of people gainfully employed. Once I drafted a letter, which went all the way up the chain and off without any redrafting at all. It was to a lady who was worried about the effects on her goldfish of radioactive effluent in the River Thames – or something like that. This was such a rare occurrence that people stopped me in the corridor to congratulate me for days afterwards. "That was a good letter you wrote about levels of radioactive effluent in the River Thames", they'd say.

Perhaps, before going any further, I should say a word or two about these secrets. I wouldn't like anyone to think that the MRC were cavalier enough to let real Grade A secrets loose in London with me and Dave Harwood and a little old man in a plain van. Although they were treated with great caution and respect and kept in pink files marked X and XX and only hands that had signed the Official Secrets Act could be laid upon them, they never really lived up to expectations. There was better value to be had from a file in the "A" series labelled CRANKS, which had letters from people convinced that their drainpipes were being invaded by plankton from outer space. The X files were mostly military secrets from the First World War – diet sheets for soldiers in the trenches; sanitary arrangements for men in armour-plated tanks; that sort of thing. I say "that sort of thing" but of course it wasn't exactly that sort of thing. I can't tell you exactly what sort of thing because I'm still bound by the Official Secrets Act, but the unnerving thing is that so totally unmemorable were they that I couldn't if I wanted to and even worse, because I can't remember what they were I may, purely by chance, have done so. I did once, after a disappointing rainy morning spent with a few of these files, tax Sir with the undramatic quality of his secrets. He considered this for a while and then said, "They might not start a Third World War, but we wouldn't like the *Daily Express* to get at them", which has always seemed to me to be a very fine definition of a secret.

Anyway, there we were one September Saturday morning: Dave Harwood and I with this plain van driven by a septuagenarian in a black uniform and peaked hat. He unlocked the back of his van for us and took down a small raffia-covered stool, about 9 inches square, for use as a step. Then he stayed in the back of the van arranging the files in piles as Dave Harwood and I and the lady from the Registry trotted out with them.

Now, when the van was loaded, we found ourselves with a problem. Our instructions from Sir had been explicit. We were, personally, to travel with the files, keeping them under our surveillance and away from the beady eyes of any marauding *Daily Express* reporter, all the way from Old Queen Street to Park Crescent. But we both lived in Hampstead. I had travelled in by car and to abandon this in Westminster and then end up in Regents Park, halfway to Hampstead, without it, seemed to us unnecessarily inconvenient. Also, the back of the van was dusty and there was nowhere to sit except the raffia stool. But the British Civil Servant is trained to use his initiative and make speedy decisions in times of crisis and, after some thought and consultation, Dave and I decided that the spirit of our briefing would, in fact, be better met if we were to follow in the car, where we could at least spot the *Daily Express* men closing in, rather than in the van itself where, as it was pitch-dark and windowless, we might be taken by surprise.

The old man took a fairly obvious route, up Whitehall, Charing Cross Road, Oxford Street, and Upper Regent Street. Dave Harwood and I would have preferred something a bit more cloak and dagger ourselves: perhaps cutting up alongside the National Gallery and through Leicester Square and making a final unexpected approach from the West along Marylebone Road, but we realised that we were only amateurs at the game. Halfway up the Charing Cross Road the van stopped and the old man got out, inspected his nearside back tyre carefully and got back in again. Apart from that the drive passed without incident.

25

We had various affairs of our own to attend to when we reached the new offices, before unpacking the van, such as checking on our accommodation. There was the matter of a carpet, which I was anxious to resolve. Of course, I was far too junior to be entitled to a carpet in my office, but rumour had it that I was to share with a woman who, although not strictly entitled to one either, had through some quirk of the system occupied a carpeted office for the last 11 years. The general opinion was that the rigidities of the Civil Service would bend rather than dispossess a lady of a carpet of 11 years' standing.

The office, when I found it, was indeed carpeted and I was also pleased to see that my typewriter was there too. Although I was too junior for a carpet, as an Executive Officer I was too senior to be allowed to type and I had suffered from this in my first months in the MRC, having illegible handwriting and being third in line for the typist – after the SMO and MO, but before the CO. I had solved the problem by finding a vast and apparently unused machine in somebody else's office and pinching it. The Clerical Officer disapproved of this on a great many points of principle and I had been afraid that she would use the opportunity of the move to manoeuvre it away, in spite of the large label with my name on which I had tied to it.

Altogether everything looked highly satisfactory so I returned to the van. Dave Harwood had efficiently unlocked the Registry and the Registry lady was in situ ready to receive the files.

The little old man shuffled round and unlocked the back of the van, took out his raffia stool and set it carefully in the road. Stepping in, he picked up an armful of XXs, stood unsteadily at the edge of the van, with his left leg hovering uncertainly over the raffia stool. With great deliberation he lowered his foot exactly one half inch to the left of the stool, catching his ankle a resounding crack on the frame and precipitating himself in a cascade of pink files and white paper into the middle of Park Crescent. A gentle breeze caught the priceless secrets of World Wars I and II and, for all I know, the Boer War and the Crimea and fluttered them softly in the direction of Regent's Park. But England being what it is, in no time at all a small crowd had gathered and was down on its hands and knees in the road, helpfully harvesting what it could.

Here Dave Harwood and I were faced with the kind of decision no Civil Servant should be called upon to make in the absence of his Master. Should we go around diligently stamping on the fingers of these good citizens as they sifted through the gutters, on the off chance that one of them might be a *Daily Express* reporter cunningly disguised as a Russian spy and the near certainty that none of them was security cleared? In the end – and I still feel we were right – we took the soft option. We said thanks very much and joined them in the gutter. We avoided each other's eyes whenever anyone paused to sit up and read out a funny bit, and before long all was safely gathered in, more or less. If it was less nobody ever complained to us about it. Perhaps they never even noticed.

* *Chapman Pincher was a Daily Express Journalist who became famous for his pursuit of traitors and supposed traitors in the British secret service.*

DOMESTIC BLISS
IN THE NHS

6

Home is a sheltered environment

The peripatetic life of a junior houseman may not suit everyone, but it has its advantages if you look in the right places. If you can't get a mortgage, join the psychiatric service, tell yourself that worldly ambition is just another neurotic trait, and head for a lovely provincial mental hospital. The accommodation is cheap and palatial and you live in an unaccustomed style of neo-Victorian elegance, with a cast of hundreds to do your housework at 25p a week.

Our first hospital house had been a pub around the turn of the century and it still acted like a Swiss weather chalet. As the rain clouds and the rising mist gathered over Epping Forest, a strong, unmistakable smell of beer rose from the cellars and seeped into the sitting room. A sizeable, unkempt property it was, but with it we inherited Charlie, who had worked for the previous inhabitants for 15 years and whose domestic expertise was, it soon became apparent to both of us, so superior to mine that there was no question about who should run the house. "We always keep the cleaning things here," he said, rather reproachfully, shifting them from under the sink to a quiet corner of the larder. He knew exactly what kind of polish went on the four-foot square of red quarry tiles in the kitchen and bought a 5 lb tin of it wholesale – he'd worked for a consultant before and wasn't too familiar with the average span of a Junior House Officer's appointment. Charlie was what they call a burnt-out schizophrenic and, within the sheltered environment of the hospital, he was a lot more normal as far as we could see than most of the staff in the same environment.

We had a happy time together, Charlie and I, that first three months. When he wasn't polishing the tiles he was helping me to slosh white and terracotta paint around the house, disguising the off-cream and green colour scheme so beloved of Hospital Secretaries everywhere. (That's another side-benefit of the peripatetic life – by the time you settle down after a half-dozen or so moves you may have got some of the more bizarre decorative ideas out of your system.) He used to bring me little presents too, from time to time, bought at jumble sales. "I've got this for you," he'd say, handing me Peter Scott birds in a passe-partout frame with cracked glass. "It cost half-a-crown," and I'd add the two shillings and sixpence to his week's wages.

Things changed a little after the baby was born. He preferred taking her for walks to polishing the tiles, and everything got a bit sloppy around the house. "I did the nappies for you, Mrs F," he told me proudly one day, when I came home to find the place stinking like a Piccadilly underground lavatory at cleaning time. There was a half-empty bottle of Jeyes fluid on the washing machine. "You have to be very careful about germs with babies," he explained.

But, come the summer, even the baby paled into insignificance. There was an awful lot of grass around that house; enough for two good-sized croquet lawns and a round of clock-golf. In about March, when it all started to grow in an abandoned fashion, we started negotiations with the hospital about whether, seeing that we were living in a hospital house surrounded by hospital grass, we were entitled to use the hospital motor-mower to keep it all under control. It seemed a reasonable enough proposition to us, but after a while we began to feel like Washington making overtures to Hanoi. Have you ever made a waxen image of a Hospital Secretary? In the end we bought a Suffolk Colt, which proved a bit of an embarrassment in our next hospital accommodation, a two-roomed fifth-floor flat behind Oxford Street, but Charlie loved it and all summer he was out there mowing every afternoon. We had the smoothest croquet lawns in Essex and I took my own baby for walks.

Charlie wasn't the only help we had, either. There was Diana, known to the hospital wives as Lady Di because she was so much more refined than we were. She dropped in when the fancy took her to do the ironing and for some reason the going rate for her was twice Charlie's. I didn't mind; she was a great ego-booster to have around: my husband said she was the only person he'd ever met who ironed his shirts worse than I did. She worked in Boots on her on days, and very dark and scornful she was. I wouldn't have liked to ask her for anything indelicate.

We had a bit of help with the garden, too, on top of Charlie and the mower. My mother once looked out of the window and saw a male ward in its entirety marching up the path, armed to the teeth with a fearsome array of apparently martial instruments. We found her later, locked in the bathroom, her first-born grandchild clutched to her breast. That was only a one-offspring working party though: the regular gardeners were a manic-depressive pair called Fred and William. William was sad and silent – I never heard him speak – but Fred did the communicating for both of them. With his tea at elevenses each day he would render 20 minutes solid of faintly familiar, blankish verse, which I took to be the more obscure bits of Tamburlaine until, listening more carefully one morning, I realized it was all his own and better nonsense than Lear ever wrote. He used to sing, too.

Can you wonder that I haven't bothered with domestic help since? Thirty-five pence an hour and none of them sing. I can't bring myself to do it. I did have a Mrs Parker for a while last year – a friend in the Welfare wanted to find her a job; her husband was in jail and she was feeling a bit low. "It's the company she needs," my friend explained, "but you'll have to be careful – she tires very easily and she's not strong. And don't mention prisons either. She's very sensitive."

Mrs P's husband obviously hadn't got the makings of a master criminal. He and his mate had discovered a few bottles of beer in the factory that they were burgling, and the police picked them up on the steps outside, an hour or so later, stoned to the eyebrows and surrounded by swag. I could see why she felt sensitive. The first day she came she spent two hours cleaning the bathroom, while I chatted to her through the door so she wouldn't be lonely and carried buckets up and down the stairs so she wouldn't get tired. Don't jump to conclusions about Mrs P's workmanship. Our bathroom's worth two hours of anybody's time. The bath is one of the free-standing kind, with appealing little feet, and what collects all soddenly behind it is too sordid to go into. Anyone else would have it out and full of daffodil bulbs in a flash, but there is within the family a school of thought, which holds that it is a period piece in keeping with the property and must be protected. That bath has done more for the cause of Women's Lib around here than Germaine Greer.

Charlie was upset when we moved on at the end of the year, and so were we. A decorating team moved in as soon as we moved out, stripping off the terracotta and the montage in the kitchen and painting it all nicely cream and green again. The next tenant was a Senior House Officer who didn't keep Charlie on – his wife didn't think he'd be safe with the children. I felt quite sorry that I'd left her all that polish in the larder.

We didn't realise it at the time (1963), but we were one of the last generation to have the kind of experience I describe here. The 1959 Mental Health Act and the 1962 Hospital Plan presaged the closing of the old mental hospitals and the assimilation of psychiatric care into the wider hospital system. But it was not until the 1970s that both Labour and Conservative governments acknowledged the need to provide more resources to deliver mental health services in the community. After the introduction of Care in the Community in the early 1980s, Warley Hospital went into a period of decline and eventually closed in 2001. I often wondered what happened to Charlie and Lady Di and all the others. I hope they did receive the care in the community that they needed.

7

Stability begins at home

~~

The psychiatrist's wife, like a hypomanic girl guide, smiles and sings under all difficulties. She has to, poor girl. Her husband watches her like Mata Hari for the least sign of neurosis, hissing whenever she bites her fingernails and muttering "your role is to stabilise the home" on her off days. He maintains the same calm, reasoned attitude towards his children, too, IQ testing them on each birthday, and working over their emotional development with their teachers at school Open Evenings. "Does she relate warmly to her peers?" he demands, and that's just the beginning.

The staff are used to all sorts; they can usually cope, but one look at the other parents, standing by to discuss their offspring's reading ability and you know you'll never be elected to the PTA.

I have heard it said, surprisingly often in fact, that psychiatrists don't discipline their children. This sadly widespread view is due to a misunderstanding by the layman of the psychopathological characteristics necessary for a comfortable life. Naturally we were both determined that our children should not grow up like their mother, with such an unhealthy regard for authority that they cry when admonished by policemen or make immoderately inconvenient arrangements for cashing cheques at the off-licence, because of an obsessional fear that behind every bank clerk lurks a manager, eager to discuss their overdraft. It's the Bad Fairy at the christening who bestows a super-abundance of Super Ego, and we're only trying to keep her at bay.

When we became parents we realised the immense importance of answering all questions with complete honesty. The trouble is, they never ask the right questions. They seldom sit wide-eyed before you saying, "Daddy, how did the world begin?" They shake you awake at 3.30 a.m. demanding, "Did Guy Fawkes have trouble with his socks?" or "Do robbers wear hats?" – questions to which an adequate answer cannot easily be dragged out of the vile pre-dawn. But, of course, there are times when we come into our own. I don't know about the rest of you, but my own formal sex education was confined to an occasion known as Dr Brown's Leaving Lecture. Dr Brown was a maiden lady of indeterminate age and sex whose secrets, imparted to each generation of girls before thrusting them upon a randy world, were jealously guarded by the recipients, in spite of close examination afterwards. I found this attitude selfish and incomprehensible until the day of my own enlightenment dawned. Dr Brown skirted delicately around the edges of our ignorance for 40 minutes, leaving us sadder, but no wiser, an almost incredible feat, cleverly achieved by the careful vagueness of her phraseology.

"Sex is a Golden Thread running through our lives," I remember her saying, and "Sex is a High-Powered Car and Alcohol lets the brakes off." "Any Questions?" she asked at the end, but we were all a bit disillusioned by this time, and also doubtful as to how fast the Golden Thread had run through Dr Brown's own life, so we let the moment pass. A fine turn of phrase she had, and fearful ignorance is a powerful contraceptive, so few of us were drummed out of the Old Girls' Guild for untimely pregnancies.

That was all very well in its way, but hardly suitable for a psychiatrist's family. How awful if they grew up ignorant, or guilty, or misinformed. How lucky that they have had so sound a grounding so early. Why, only the other day I heard our 3-year-old son giving a pretty impressive bath-time lecture to a visiting 18-month-old (poor kid, her father's an anaesthetist, she hadn't been told a thing). "I have a penis and you haven't," he was telling her, "because you're not a boy - yet."

We have our anxious moments, but we never let them show.

"Mummy, Mummy, Miss Francis talked to the WHOLE SCHOOL today."

"Really dear?"

"Some boys did SOMETHING TERRIBLE."

Doubts start to form.

"They did it in the lavatories." Ah well, boys will be boys.

"They did it in the GIRLS' lavatory." Doubts begin to crystallize.

"They did it to one of the girls. It was to Jacynth. She was still crying at home time."

Rape before seven, God knows what by eleven. Can we possibly afford a transfer to the private, ladies-only seminary round the corner and be damned to our principles and the State? Better get her to talk it all out though, communicate her fears. "Er, what exactly did they do to poor Jacynth, dear?"

"They climbed over the partition and SPAT at her."

They will have their hang-ups, no doubt about that, but these are more likely to centre round the deathbed than the marriage-bed. "Oh, what a pretty wedding," ours sentimentally say as the beflowered corteges go daily by on their way to the South London crematorium, and I haven't the heart to disillusion them. It's DAD in red roses on top of the coffin that seizes me up somehow, and I hurry them, eyes averted, past the mummies in the British Museum too. But you can't protect them from everything, and I haven't yet found a way to avoid those heart-breaking conversations over trays of chops in butchers' shops, leading step by inevitable step to the final, incredulous, "But don't the little lambs' mummies mind?" Ah well, they will have some terrible death-bed scenes. I can see it all . . . "But Mother never told me it would be like this". "Just lie back, close your eyes, and think of England" . . . A Golden Oscar to the first primary school to teach the kids the Facts of Death.

8

Nothing like a good night's sleep

~

My mother-in-law's penchant for picking up lame ducks was unequalled even by Noah. She also has red hair and a will far stronger than mine, so I didn't argue too much when she told us about Rosie. That's the trouble with this profession – to every man his own GP but the catchment area of the psychiatrist extends far beyond the confines of Camberwell Green to include his friends, his relations, their friends and relations, and all the women he sits next to at dinner parties. Their eyes light up as he sits down beside them, and they start off coy and nervous, but I can tell by the glazed look in his eye and the way their husbands are shifting in their seats that the psyches are well unravelled by the second course, and afterwards they confide, "It must be lovely being married to a psychiatrist. I suppose he knows everything you're thinking." Madam, if only you knew.

But let's get back to my mother-in-law. She had been undergoing traction for a broken femur for the last four months at a hospital somewhere in the Scottish outback where Rosie was one of the ward orderlies. They had apparently set up a satisfactory symbiotic relationship, with Rosie supplying such comforts as were not readily available on the Health Service – cups of tea and hot water bottles – while my mother-in-law exchanged sympathy for the tea, together with her own brand of homespun psychotherapy. She kept us fully informed on all stages of Rosie's life and hard times – apart from drinking tea there wasn't a lot else she could do in her position – and we saw the transference developing, letter by letter, before our very eyes.

So it was hardly any surprise at all to get the final letter, just as she was about to come and convalesce with us. Rosie, my mother-in-law told us, was a really lovely person, and so kind. But she had been working much, much too hard. And she had this terrible sleep problem. Why, sometimes she'd hardly close her eyes for nights on end and then of course she couldn't do her job properly and Sister wasn't very understanding, you know. What she needed was a nice, relaxing holiday. And she'd be such a help with the children (two pretty contradictory statements there, I thought, but never mind). And, continued my mother-in-law, with the air of one producing an irresistible white rabbit from the depths of her bed jacket, Peter would be able to, you know, talk to her in the evenings, and that would do Rosie such a lot of good.

Isn't it marvellous what the fairy god-analyst can achieve through sheer sleight of tongue? Mind you, there are those who don't subscribe to this enchanting view of the psychiatrist as something between John the Baptist and the Wizard of Oz. They think they are all mad. Well now, there's an absurd hypothesis. Look around our hospital canteen any day of the week and a more normal bunch of manic-depressives you couldn't hope to see. Let's nip this one smartly in the bud and keep our lingering doubts to ourselves, shall we?

We met the Scottish recovery team at Euston early one morning. They had been escorted down by my sister-in-law, normally a woman of some poise and beauty, but she looked pretty haggard just then. She had shared a second-class sleeper with Rosie, who had kept them both awake all night doing what was evidently the Scottish Presbyterian equivalent of telling one's beads. Rosie herself, whey-faced and carrying a small tartan bag, trotted down the platform repeating, not entirely sotto voce, "I should niver hae come". Of the party, only my mother-in-law, be-crutched as she was on either side, showed any signs of *joie de vivre*. She always travels first class.

We didn't see much of Rosie for the next 48 hours. She was evidently catching up on her sleep. Occasionally she appeared for meals, though whether for social or nutritional reasons it was difficult to say. "Is she real?" asked one of the children in wonderment after several attempts at communication had failed, and I saw what he meant. She had the faintly trance-like, otherworldly air that one has come to associate with American astronauts, Mr Spock, and other characters from outer space. Neither did she eat. Like Pooh with Tigger, I spent some time trying to discover what it was that Rosie liked, but eventually she evolved a diet to her own satisfaction, of tea and toast at three-hourly intervals, and I felt that its vitamin content was none of my business. I offered to take her to see Buckingham Palace but she didn't seem too keen. Perhaps she was a Scottish Nationalist. By the end of the second day, even my mother-in-law was showing signs of strain. "I think I'll give her half a Soneryl at bedtime," she said, "a really good night would make all the difference in the world to her."

"How did you sleep, Rosie?" I asked brightly when she shuffled down at 11.15 next morning. "Ah, terrible, terrible," she moaned, settling down at the kitchen table for a cup of tea and a quiet nap. She might not manage a wink at night, but she was as soporific as a Flopsy Bunny on lettuce during the day.

My mother-in-law had intimated that Rosie would be delighted to baby-sit for us at any time, so that evening, with some misgivings, we left her sitting, swaying slightly, in the middle of the playroom floor while the children ran amok around her. They didn't look fairly matched, but we went out all the same. When we got home the house was silent, except for the snores of Rosie, who lay prone and unrousable upon the sitting-room floor. Together we heaved her up the stairs, arguing bitterly about who was better qualified to put her to bed, my husband by virtue of his profession or me on account of my sex. Then we tackled my mother-in-law. "I did give her two," she said, a shade defensively, "because I thought it was so important for her to get some sleep. I suppose they can knock you out rather if you're not used to them."

"I think," said my husband next morning, putting on his coat, "that you'd better search her room. Naturally," he added, opening the door, "I'd help you. But unfortunately it's my clinic morning."

I lured Rosie downstairs with tea and toast as soon as she was conscious and made a ladylike sortie through her possessions. There seemed to be quantities of aspirin and codeine bottles and one labelled sodium amytal, which I impounded and gave to my mother-in-law, with instructions to administer them sparsely. She was still rather shaken by the previous night's episode and promised to have a little talk with Rosie. She felt sure nothing like that would ever happen again.

The next morning Rosie didn't appear at all, so at lunchtime I went up to her room. She was sitting unsteadily on the edge of her bed, a codeine bottle in one hand, four Soneryl in the other. "Now, now, Rosie, I'm sure you've had enough," I said, making a grab for the bottle. She didn't stand a chance, used as I am to wresting Smarties from three-year-olds. (Whoever said it was easy, taking candy from a child? Had they ever tried it?) Then she cunningly keeled over into total unconsciousness, knocking the bottle out of my hand and catching it before it hit the floor. So I went downstairs to telephone the hospital, calling in at my mother-in-law's room to suggest that she might like to have another little chat with Rosie.

My husband was home at the double, and we tore upstairs to find her sitting beside Rosie, patting her hand. She was saying, sounding just a touch this side of hysterical, "She's tired. She's tired. She's very, very tired. You know what it's like when you can't get a good night's sleep."

That's the nice thing about my mother-in-law: she always believes the best of everyone. As for Rosie, she had a nice, relaxing holiday in the drug addiction unit.

9

Rich, not gaudy

~

M y husband is lucky enough to be the owner of a very fine overcoat. He has owned it for some time – we met when we were twenty and the coat was young. It was an elegant, jaunty coat with spring in its pile, a fashionable, black coat, which might be worn with confidence almost anywhere. Now, nearly twenty years later, its coal-black nap is rubbed and worn and has acquired a greenish tinge and time has separated its seams. Patches of mould appear around the pockets after a summer hanging in the cellar and the swagger in its skirts is caused less by its youthful cut and vigour than by the lack of stitching in the back vent. But it is still, I think my grandfather would have said, a good piece of cloth. My grandfather was a cotton manufacturer and much interested in the quality of his acquaintances' clothing. He was, so I am told, in the habit of picking small threads from the hems of ladies' dresses and setting fire to them, though I forget exactly why.

The coat has an interesting cut. It swirls halfway between his knees and his ankles and gives him, so I have always thought, a romantic, dashing look. It is known within the family as Napoleon. It would be unthinkable, after all we have been through together, to send such an overcoat to the knacker's yard; to parcel it up, as some have suggested we should, and give it to a jumble sale or Oxfam, or even despatch it to a quiet Mediterranean island to see out the twilight of its life.

The coat, as I have said, was a fashionable coat back in 1954. It came from a good tailor: a tailor recommended by my husband's brother-in-law, who knows about such things and sets great store by them, who advised him, when he went to university, to have his hair cut at Trumpers and open a bank account at Coutts. But such is the fickleness of human nature that it was this same brother-in-law, twenty years later, who refused to allow my husband to attend the confirmation service of his nephew wearing this same overcoat. He substituted instead an overcoat of his own and we have a photograph of the confirmation party outside the school chapel, my husband looking strange and faintly uncomfortable in this smart, alien overcoat, which sits squarely on his shoulders and falls well short of his knees.

The overcoat enjoyed a brief renewed vogue during the time that Dr Zhivago was filmed and the glances it attracted were once more glances of admiration, even envy. It did, in fact, once visit Russia one November, though not upon my husband's shoulders. A friend who had to make an unexpected visit to Leningrad found his own wardrobe inadequate and thought immediately of Napoleon. I should have liked to have seen it strolling through the grounds of the Winter Palace, a coat in its natural environment come into its own at last.

It is odd, when one thinks of the affection with which we regard the coat, to realise that it is an object of derision in other people's eyes. It has earned him the titles, successively and in several different hospitals of the Worst Dressed Junior House Officer, Senior House Officer, Junior Registrar and Senior Registrar and there are those among our friends who have expressed the fear that such unparalleled apparel might even prevent his final metamorphosis. They buttonholed me about it over lunch at the hospital one day.

"What is he going to wear for his interview?" demanded Ruth.

"Well," I said, "He'll wear his interview suit. And the tie with the little pink diamonds on it if you don't think it's too frivolous. And I've bought him a new shirt so that the corners of his collar won't turn up. Will that do?"

George and Ruth looked at each other.

"You are not," said Ruth, leaning over the table in a menacing fashion, "going to let him wear his overcoat?"

I felt protective and defensive, like I do when the children go to stay with my mother and she writes to tell me she's had to buy them all new vests. "Why not?" I said. "It's a perfectly good coat. There's nothing wrong with that coat. I had it relined last year. And anyway, he'll be wearing it when he gets there. If he gets there."

"Do you realise," said George, clenching his fists – and George is a mild, soft-spoken fellow, not at all given to shows of temperament or displays of strong emotion – "do you realise," he said, and gave a small shudder of horror at the memory, "that when we were in Munich last October people were standing around us at the airport laughing at him?"

Morecambe and Wise rehearse for hours to get an effect like that and he just puts his coat on.

We compromised in the end. I drove him up to the hospital for the interview and he went in with the overcoat draped inside out over his arm, heavily disguised as standard 1974 consultant wear. He didn't need actually to put it on till they'd offered him the job. But they may be relieved to know, George and Ruth, that we shall soon be able to retire Napoleon after all, because of Great Uncle Albert. Great Uncle Albert was presented to us by some friends after they had watched my husband walking to work one morning. They had inherited Great Uncle Albert from a relative of the same name and he is not dissimilar to Napoleon in cut and style. A little wider, perhaps, for Great Uncle Albert

47

was evidently a substantial man, but the same comfortable, shin-warming length. He is made of a good, solid tweed, a cloth my grandfather would have approved of. I would say he'd got at least another twenty years of wear in him yet.

10

Doctor at Law

One of the things I learnt at my father's knee (I come from a long line of lawyers) was to steer clear of litigation and keep out of court. My husband hasn't had my advantages – his mother was only a surgeon – which shows the importance of assortative mating: there are far fewer marital problems when your Walter Mitty fantasies, like your principles, run more or less in parallel.

The most dangerous dreams are those with an element of reality. Mine are about the footlights of the London Palladium, for example, and as I can't act and I can't sing and I can't dance there is only a slender chance of their ever being acted out. My husband, on the other hand, has always rather fancied himself as Perry Mason, and he had real problems when he started making regular appearances at the Old Bailey as an expert medical witness. He might not have found this as seductive if the judges he came before had given him a hard time every now and then, but most of them seemed to hold the profession in high regard and tended to defer to him and thank him profusely for giving up his valuable time to the court, which fuelled his fantasy life no end. But what finally pushed him over the edge was when I got my back bumper tangled up with the front bumper of a taxi going around Cambridge Circus and he discovered that instead of settling out of court we could fight the case ourselves in the County Court.

When we all turned up in court, about 18 months later because litigation is a lengthy business, the taxi-driver had his solicitor with him, who was carrying a small, neat briefcase. I had my husband, who had cancelled his outpatient clinic and was carrying my defence. This consisted of several large sheets of paper with scale diagrams worked out in the hospital car park to show the turning circle of our car, a plastic ice-cream carton containing a series of little matchbox cars to add three-dimensional verisimilitude to the diagrams, and a few photographs of the car itself and of me with a tape-measure trying to measure the width of Cambridge Circus in the middle of the traffic and looking very embarrassed, as indeed I was. We also had a very young apprentice barrister, the pupil of a friend of ours, who'd been sent along because our friend thought it would be educational for him. The taxi-driver sat on the plaintiff's side of the court and we settled down on the other, respectably separated like friends of the bride and groom.

The judge was a tetchy lady with a disconcerting habit of burying her face in her hands as though anxious to get away from it all when anyone said anything she disapproved of, which was quite often. Within a very short time she had reduced both me and the taxi-driver to nervous idiocy by pouncing on various grey areas and inconsistencies in our respective accounts of the incident, which I at any rate thought she might have made allowances for, seeing as how the whole thing had happened so long ago. We cast each other glances of sympathy and both of us started backtracking a bit to corroborate each other's story, which made her crosser than ever. I'd have called the whole thing off and settled there and then if it hadn't been for my husband sitting there so eager and well prepared.

When his turn came he sprang up and spread all his evidence on a table in front of the judge who buried her head in her hands again. Then he explained about the turning properties of Volkswagen vans and proved how impossible it was for me to have hooked my bumper into the taxi's by cutting in front of him, as he said I did, but that it could have happened if I'd been turning left down the Charing Cross Road, as I said I was, and he'd been far too close to me, as he said he wasn't. It was complex, but impressive. After a while the apprentice barrister passed me a note which read 'I don't think this judge is very mechanically minded. I'm not at all sure she's following your husband's line of argument.' After a while she lifted up her head and said testily, 'Just a minute, just a minute. What are you? Are you an engineer?'

'No,' said my husband.

'Well then,' said the judge, 'What do you do?'

'I'm a psychiatrist,' he said. She probably woke several times in the night thinking of the witty ripostes she might have made to that, but at the time she was lost for words.

However, in her summing up she recovered a little *joie de vivre* and was nice to us all. She said that the taxi-driver and I were both honest and intelligent witnesses although she believed that one of us was mistaken in her memory of the event. She said that my husband was a man loyally springing to his wife's aid and congratulated him on the work he'd put into his defence, which she described as ingenious. Then she found for the taxi-driver and said we'd have to pay £15 costs.

Afterwards the taxi-driver and I shook hands and said we hoped if we met again it would be in happier circumstances: happier for me that is. Then he said he'd been interested to hear about my husband's profession because his wife had a bit of a problem, so my husband quickly switched persona and gave him a good deal more than £15 worth of advice. In his euphoric state he'd have given anyone a free hand-out. As he said, £15 is a small price to pay for the hire of a courtroom in central London for a whole morning, with a judge and court officials thrown in. It occurs to me that the NHS could probably turn many an honest penny by providing a similar service for people whose secret lives involve Dr Kildare, an operating table and a set of assorted scalpels.

THE PROS AND CONS OF
PARENTHOOD

11

Conversations with my children

D r R D Laing,* as astute as ever, took to writing down
(and subsequently publishing) his conversations with
his children so that he could "observe the emotional
and cognitive development of two children with unimpaired
faculties unfold . . ."

It's no use the rest of us kicking ourselves because we didn't
think of doing it, or rather, it's no use if the children are over
the age of nine, because by then their faculties have become
impaired and their cognition developed and you can wait for
ever for them to say delightful things like Dr Laing's Adam,
who wants a long pole "to knock down the sun and break it
in two and give Mummy it to cook and we'll eat it".

For a week or so I have been following the children around,
notebook at the ready, as a keen gardener might follow a horse,

and to discourage anyone else from wasting time doing the same I publish the results below. Let us trace the development of three children one stage further, as they worm their way out of the cosiness of early childhood into the dawn of adolescence with its deeper preoccupations, its wider vision and its growing awareness that the reason parents tend not to go around barefoot is that they know their clay feet are showing.

I hate her; she's always borrowing my plimsolls.
I hate her; she's always pinching my pen.
I hate her; she's always using my hairbrush.
I hate her; she never feeds the cats.

He's always watching television; why don't you stop him?
He never goes to bed at the right time; why don't you make him?
He always finishes off the biscuits; why do you let him?

Polly's mother makes the most wonderful picnics. She gives us hard-boiled eggs and raw carrots.
Yes, I know I've always said I didn't like them, but Polly's mother's hard-boiled eggs are much nicer than your hard-boiled eggs.
Polly's mother always uses wholemeal brown flour; your pastry might be a bit better if you did that.
Polly's mother knitted her this fantastic sweater and it only took her three evenings and Polly's going to bring the pattern to school tomorrow so that you can do me one so I could wear it on Saturday.
Polly's mother lets the guinea pigs come into her bed.
Polly's mother never gets cross.

I've got an invitation to a disco party.
No, of course I'm not going; it's from a boy.
Well, I might go if Frances goes.
I could go if I had a petticoat with a frill that showed under my skirt.

What would a boy my age want for a birthday present?

She's lovely; she's a palomino about 15 hands with a bit of cob and a bit of Connemara. That's why she's such a good jumper and I wouldn't be surprised if there wasn't some Arab in her somewhere. She's got a lovely nature; of course she tries it on a bit at first because she's full of character. You've got to know how to handle her and they'll always take advantage of you until they realise you're not going to let them get away with it. I rode her in a running martingale and a loose-ring Snaffle.

If you sold our car and granny's car we could buy a Land Rover and that would be much easier for pulling a horsebox.

Yes, I know we haven't got one but we'll have to get one some time.

When you come to Open Evening you can talk to Miss Roberts and Mr Edgar and Mr Morrison but you can't talk to Mr Forest because I don't like him and you can't talk to Mrs Vines because she doesn't like me. And you're not to talk to Mr Welsh.

I'm not going to tell you why. Just don't talk to him, that's all.

You didn't want it did you?

You weren't saving it were you?

Well, how was I to know it was for tomorrow's supper?

You owed me eight weeks pocket money and two weeks cookery money and that £1 I lent you and I've taken it out of your bag but I put back the 10p I owed you so you've got about 25p left. Is that all right?

What I'd really like for Christmas is a radio-controlled aeroplane. You can get it in Hamleys. It costs £150. It could be for my birthday too . . .

Mrs Evans says you shouldn't wear jeans when you're mountain climbing because if it rains and they get wet they'll shrink and that could be dangerous.

Mrs Evans says she's been married twice and she doesn't think it's worth bothering again so next time she's just going to live with the chap.

Mrs Evans knows this man and he lost three fingers in an accident and someone found them in the gutter and took them to hospital and they stitched them back on and now he's a concert pianist.

Mrs Evans is having to leave next term because she hasn't taught us enough history.

You didn't get to university, did you? I don't *believe* it.

When you stand like that your tummy sticks out.

Now you're getting on a bit you ought to wear your hair in a little bun at the back like great-granny used to.

I don't want Daddy to come to Founder's Day Service. He might sing.

* *R D Laing was a pioneering psychiatrist who blamed parents for the psychological problems of their offspring. But as a father, he was depressed, alcoholic and often cruel.*

12

Out of the mouths

The children came home from school singing a merry little song one day:

As we go marching two by two,
He slept with me, I slept with you.

"Would you mind repeating that?" I said. I know primary education is full of surprises nowadays, but I thought that was a bit borderline for a good Church school.

"We got it off the BBC," they told me, "it's a marching song." Ah, those dear, dead Aldermaston days.

At the end of term they brought the words home. They went like this:

As we go marching two by two,
Keep step with me, I'll step with you.

That's the trouble with pornography. When you get down to the hard core it tends to disappoint. But you can understand why my mother-in-law feels that the quality of life is changing. We took her and the children to see *Live and Let Die*. The children dived under the seats in horror during the title sequences and had to be taken out, and every time there was any sex or violence my mother-in-law muttered, "Why do they have make films like this when there are so many beautiful things in the world?" I'd have enjoyed it on my own.

"Did you hear what That Boy said this morning?"

My mother-in-law nodded in the general direction of the hall, where her grandson was busy laying railway track. It had been a peaceful holiday afternoon until then, with me reading, her sewing and the girls playing Monopoly.

I had heard, but I didn't let on. I knew she wouldn't be able to bring herself to repeat it. His sisters had no such scruples.

"He said fucking knickers," they chorused smugly.

I pantomimed horror and amazement nicely mingled with shame and apology but this was obviously not enough. "I'll speak to him about it," I said.

My mother-in-law didn't reply, so I edged myself gently back into my book. After a while she said, "Of course, he doesn't know what it *means*. You ought to tell him what it means. If he knew what it *meant*," she went on with what she evidently felt was flawless reasoning, "then he wouldn't *say* it."

"What does it mean?" asked one of the girls. Nobody answered her. I was still searching around for an uncontroversial topic when my mother-in-law said:

"What I can't understand is where he can have picked it up. He must have heard somebody say it."

I said, "Well, you know, there's television, and books..."

"He can't read," said my mother-in-law.

I put down my book. "Would you like a game of backgammon?" I asked.

We played a couple of games and then she said, "Of course, he can't have got it from his father. I'm quite, quite certain that the children have never heard either of you use it. I'm not suggesting that for a minute."

"Of course not," I said. "I didn't for a minute think you were suggesting that."

"My children never heard their father swear," she said.

I found that hard to believe. From all other accounts my father-in-law had been a colourful personality. There was a family story about him chasing his youngest son round the dining-room table with a carving knife, but perhaps he did it in dead silence.

After dinner my mother-in-law said: "I've been thinking about it. He must have learned it from somebody at That School."

That served me right for deliberately rubbing her up the wrong way the other evening on the subject of state education versus private schools. I may perhaps have given her a false impression when I was loftily expounding the advantages of bringing up the children in a mixed environment, surrounded by all classes, colours, and creeds. I wish, now, that I had told her the truth, which is that our particular state school, cosily tucked away in an impregnable middle-class ghetto, is about as mixed as Eton, thus enabling us to have our sloppily thought-out radical principles and eat them.

Anyway, I had a word with my son at bedtime that night.

"You know what you said this morning. It really shocked Granny. Some words one just has to learn not to use, even if you hear other people say them. Try not to do it again, won't you?"

He thought this over for a bit.

"I'll say vests next time," he suggested. "She won't mind that, will she?"

13

Playing up

～

Sir Henry Newbolt, accustomed as he was to the public school way of doing things, might have found himself at a loss for words had he been able to attend the Oval with me to watch the finals of the South London eight-a-side junior cricket competition.

The school was (in retrospect) over-confident. Morden Court, we were assured by a dozen small boys, sticking their heads through the school railings to chat to us, were a duff side. The cup was as good as sitting on the shelf in the headmaster's study. One mother was heard to say that she devoutly hoped this was true, as she had persuaded her husband to abandon lunch with a cabinet minister on the grounds that he might never again see his son captaining the winning side at the Oval. There was to be a medal for each member of the winning team, and – some compensation for Morden Court – tea for both teams in the Long Room at the Oval afterwards.

At the gate, Mrs Porter the French mistress handed out broadsheets explaining the game to those parents who had volunteered to transport supporters to the ground.

The rules of eight-a-side are untraditional but serve their purpose admirably. Each of four pairs of batsmen bats for three overs. Every time a wicket falls, two runs are deducted, but the pair carry on batting. At the end of their three overs they are given a bonus of twenty runs, plus however many they have made themselves, minus two for each wicket taken. It is thus quite possible for a minus score to appear on the board and, indeed, this sometimes happens, to the confusion of parents who have not studied Mrs Porter's leaflet. While two of the team are batting, another pair act as fielders for the opposing side and a third pair take the field as additional umpires, a system some might think wide open to corruption. The point of all this is to make sure a) that the match lasts no longer than the one and a half hours available, b) that everybody has a turn at the wicket, c) that there is virtually no possibility of a draw and d) that no more than two boys are left alone for any length of time to raid orchards, beat each other up, mutilate little girls or whatever else small unoccupied boys do to pass the time.

The queue of children hoping for lifts stretched right round the playground. Siblings of players and ticket holders had priority: to qualify for a ticket one must have supported other, less enticing matches on Saturday afternoons throughout the season. Ticket holders were more or less confined to fourth year boys who hoped to catch Mr Henry's eye and qualify for a place in the team by virtue of keenness if not cricketing prowess. Mr Henry, the sports master, unfortunately could not be with us to see his team triumph on this exciting day as he injured himself by falling off his shooting stick on Sports Day a couple of weeks ago. Any spaces left in the cars were allotted to a few fourth-year girls who fancied an afternoon out. The usual sexual apartheid operated and I drove off with my daughter sitting loftily aloof in the front seat of our minibus, and ten excited little boys discussing the school's chances in the back. Much was made of the talents of Preston, our best bat, and Pritchard, the fastest under-12 bowler in South London, before whom the Morden Court wickets were expected to crumble like cookies. From the way they talked you'd think Kerry Packer* had been hanging around the playground for weeks trying to sign them on.

It was blazingly hot. I had remembered, from last time we reached the finals, how thirsty everyone got and had come well supplied with orange squash, but I had forgotten how appallingly uncomfortable the Oval benches are and had not brought a cushion. What fanaticism must propel those who voluntarily sit on them for three days running to watch a test match? We were all crammed over at the gasworks end; the rest of the stands were empty except for a few elderly gentlemen dotted about here and there. I wondered whether they were Old Dulwich Hamlet Boys or Old Morden Court Boys, or just old boys. The fourth-year girls teetered up and down the aisles in their platform soles and sun-dresses, for we are not a strictly uniformed school, getting drinks from the Ladies down below and seeing if there was a better view (as if they cared) from the balcony above. Morden Court were arriving in droves now, neatly dressed in green and white. The headmasters had cleverly staggered our arrivals to avoid aggro and confusion on the stairs.

Out on the field, all the boys looked indistinguishable and unfamiliar in their long white flannels and floppy sun-hats. "I think that's Donald," said his mother uncertainly. "He said he was batting first. Or is he the other end?" It would be quite untrue to say that a breathless hush settled over the Oval as the first ball was bowled; but there was certainly an air of expectancy. Mingled cheers and boos rose from the rival gangs of supporters, and even the fourth-year girls, who did not pretend more than a passing interest in the game, glanced briefly at the pitch before abandoning themselves once more to some collective group giggle. A diminutive Morden Court bowler sent down a ball so fast that I did not even see it. Richard (or was it Donald?) had much the same trouble and turned in some surprise to see his wicket and bails splayed out in all directions. The Hamlet gave a loud groan and the scoreboard smartly subtracted two runs. The next ball hit Richard rather hard on his left leg and fifty or so Morden Court boys leapt up and shrieked hopefully "LB, LB", but none of the umpires took any notice. Keith beside me said eagerly "Do you think he is badly hurt?" He is not a sadistic boy, but his brother was first reserve.

Richard bravely rubbed his shin and carried on. He made a couple of runs next ball but was bowled twice more before the end of the over. The last ball he hit, but dithered around his crease too long to make anything of it. "Little fool," said Miss Ware behind us. "Could have run a couple there." Miss Ware takes the remedial class but does not have the sympathy one might expect for the underdog. "Who's your best bowler?" Keith anxiously asked a Morden Court boy. "Not him," the lad said, quick to take psychological advantage. "He's nothing." "They'll have none like Pritchard," Keith reassured me. "You just wait till you see him." There was a disturbance some rows in front, just under the edge of the overhanging balcony. A couple of Morden Court teachers rose to their feet, shaking something crossly from their skirts. Miss Ware charged upstairs to see what the fourth-year girls had been up to, but the culprits had vanished by the time she got there. I was quite relieved. It would have been a shame to mar the afternoon with unpleasantness and, besides, I could not for the moment spot my daughter anywhere. A couple of overs later the girls came sauntering down the aisle towards us, really to see if there was any orange squash left, but ostensibly to discover the score. "If you'd look at the score board you'd see it," snapped Miss Ware. "Sit down and don't wander about between overs."

By now the score was looking healthier. Preston and Pearce, the third pair, were in and punishing the bowling, scoring fours to the boundary, which was marked by a long piece of string because we were playing on a reduced pitch over to one side of the ground. By the time the fourth pair had had their three overs the score stood at 121 and the Hamlet were well pleased. With our demon bowler to come, victory seemed just a full toss away. But, alas, Pritchard is having an off day. Scarcely a wicket falls and by the time the fourth Morden Court pair go in to bat, their score is already 115. The boys are discouraged; the girls have totally lost interest and are lobbying to go home. At close of play, Morden Court have scored 132 and the Hamlet give them a full-throated, hearty boo, which the extra-enthusiastic clapping of parents and staff does nothing to drown. Driving out of the grounds we had to nose our way through a crocodile of Morden Court children, wending their way neatly to the Oval station. The ten little boys in the back gave assorted rude signs and jeers through the windows. "What terribly bad sportsmanship," I said severely. "Didn't Mr Henry teach you Cricket as well as cricket?" The boys looked mystified. "What else are we supposed to do?" one of them says at last. "They won, didn't they?" All so very unlike the dear old Eton and Harrow.

Kerry Packer was an Australian media tycoon who organised the World Series cricket competition, which ran between 1977 and 1979. After failing to gain exclusive television rights to Australia's Test matches in 1976, Packer set up his own series by secretly signing agreements with leading Australian, English, Pakistani, South African and West Indian players,

14

Ou est la plume de ma tante?

W hen I was at school you weren't allowed to do domestic science till the fifth form, and then only if you were considered too thick to learn anything much else. Our elder daughter's grammar school calls it Home Economics and they start it in the first form, beginning with egg and tomato sandwiches and working their way up to Victoria sponge in the third year. On the way up they learn about vitamins and kitchen hygiene, so that my daughter comes home and says, "I think you should give us more green vegetables and Miss Potts says you should wash the sugar bowl out every day." We've sent our second daughter to a boys' school that's just gone co-ed. They keep apologising for not having cooking facilities yet, so our daughter learns carpentry instead, which is all to the good, I think. She can make egg and tomato sandwiches and Victoria sponge too, because I taught her, and she doesn't pass remarks about the sugar bowl either.

Sometimes I think educationalists worry too much about making school a preparation for living. Living doesn't need ten years preparation, if you look at it one way. If you look at it another, ten years isn't nearly enough. School is for learning things you are never going to have the time or the inclination to tackle once you get out and start living, like quadratic equations and Boyle's Law and Caesar's Gallic Wars Book III. All the things I actually need, give or take a bit of basic literacy, I've learnt since I left school and, because necessity is a teacher with a strong right arm, I learnt them pretty quickly. The rest form a comfortable substratum of useless information that I can dig around in from time to time when I feel like it.

There are plenty of other changes, too. They don't have Prayers in the morning now; they have Assembly, which is probably a better way of describing the mixture of devotion and administration it always was anyway. Even Aunty's pen isn't what it was. They call it *un stylo* now. Or a *bic* if Aunty uses a ballpoint. And wait till you see the Latin. It deals with the daily routine of a Pompeiian household around the time of the eruption of Vesuvius. There is Caecilius, his slave Clemens, his cook Grumio, and his handmaiden Melissa, to mention only the kingpins of the series. Sometimes Caecilius gets drunk at dinner (roasted peacock usually) and falls asleep, so Grumio and Melissa creep in and finish off the wine. Caecilius goes to the barber's and the baths, and Clemens and his mates gossip about their employers. After Vesuvius erupts, finishing off Caecilius and Melissa, Quintus (did I mention Quintus? He's Caecilius's son) and Clemens move to Britain where they visit an old business friend of Caecilius who has a very demanding wife. There's a great deal more I'd like to tell you, but I think I've said enough for you to realise that it all bears more resemblance to *Up Pompeii* than to the Aeneid and probably gives a more rounded picture of Roman life than anything we ever learned.

I was very enthusiastic about the course at first; in fact even now I can hardly wait to get on to the next book which is called Medicus and follows neatly on from the last one, which ended with Quintus being badly injured in a crocodile hunt.

But I suddenly realised, the other day, that it is loosening the common cultural bonds between me and the children. If they ever mentioned a testudo I'd know they were only referring to the kind of dear little animal which crawls out of its shell to get lettuce. It's strange to think I'll be sharing family life with three people who will never know that All Gaul was divided into three parts.

There are lots of definite improvements. In English, for example – no grammar, less boring stuff about a Day in the Life of a Carrot or My Pets, and more chance to spread imaginative wings. Not that they always take it. My son arrived home from school more disconsolate than usual. "I have to write a poem for homework," he said. "About Night." The girls used to reel that sort of thing off by the page-load, no problem at all. He has writer's block at the very idea. It's not that he thinks poetry's cissy. He just can't do it.

"How shall I start?" he said.

"That's up to you," I told him. "Imagine yourself outside, in the middle of the night. How do you feel? What's happening around you? What's it like out there?"

"Dark," he said. "Nothing you can say about that."

But I must have put him in the right frame of mind, because ten minutes later he came back. "I've got the first line," he said. "'A car was driving through the night.' Is that all right?"

"That's fine," I said, "as far as it goes. Keep trying."

Some time later he came and showed me the second line. "'Both its headlights were blazing bright.'"

"You don't have to make it rhyme," I reminded him. "You don't want to get yourself bogged down in a strict rhyming scheme. It's more important to get an idea flowing. Use rhythm; use metre; find the poetry in the words themselves. That's why you're so much luckier than we were. When I was at school our poems were expected to rhyme."

"I want it to rhyme," he said firmly. "It doesn't sound like poetry if it doesn't rhyme. What shall I put next?"

"Well," I said, "that's quite an intriguing beginning you've got there. Just sit and think about this car for a few minutes. There it goes, flashing through the night, headlights blazing. What is it doing? Where's it going? Tell me some more about it."

He thought for a few minutes. Then he said, "It's a Ford Escort, four cylinders, 1200 cc with front wheel suspension and an automatic gear change."

"I meant something interesting," I said.

"It's blue," he said. You can't help them when they get into that sort of mood.

He struggled away all through *John Craven's Newsround* to produce the next line. "'It hit an owl and gave him a fright.'"

"All I want now is one more line to finish it off," he said triumphantly.

"'It would have missed him if he'd been flying six inches to the right'," said my husband.

"'I wept, grief-stricken, at his plight'," said the elder daughter.

"'The blood and feathers were a terrible sight'," said the second on

"I rather like that," said my son.

"You think of your own last line," I said. "Take no notice of them."

He finished it off at school next morning so I never saw how it ended. I bet it rhymed though. He said his teacher liked the poem and it might go in the school magazine. It's good to know there's one place where the old values are still appreciated.

15

Sitting on a powerhouse

Anyone who has ever caught himself yelling incoherently at his offspring, "Don't you shout at me like that," will know what I mean when I say that children are the victims of a shameful degree of doublethink. "Of course you can't give it up," we say, horrified, when they demand to swop recorder for piano lessons, dancing for acrobatics. We extol the virtues of perseverance, endurance, self-improvement, suppressing the niggling memories of our own abandoned attempts to learn Swahili or upholstery or the harpsichord, of the volumes of Teach Yourself this or that lying in the bookcase, unblemished by use. No reading at the table, we say, sweeping the Beano onto the floor without looking up from the Observer. You wouldn't like it, we say, stirring the coq au vin with one hand and turning the fish fingers with the other. At bath-time one day I was reprimanding a daughter for some minor breach of manners. "People just don't like children who are terribly rude and don't say please," I said, scrubbing away in emphasis. "No," she replied, with some bitterness, "And they don't like people who wash other people's knees without asking them, either."

But don't let's waste too much sympathy on the little mites. They are not as under-privileged as they sometimes lead you to believe. My children are awe-inspiring in their ability to do things I couldn't do at their age and certainly can't do now – play the guitar, climb up a rope, swim a mile – the list grows longer with every passing year and my adult supremacy less and less. Sometimes you have to be ruthless to keep your end up. Our eldest is learning chess with her father. "I didn't mean to go there," she squeals. "Give me back my queen."

"It's too late," he snaps back, "You took your finger off." That, from a man who won't play Scrabble unless he's allowed to go off the edge of the board.

And worse is to come. Infants less than a year old, I read in the Observer recently, are developing their physical and mental powers at a unique "school" for babies in Czechoslovakia. "Small babies have possibilities within them which may be lost if they are not developed within the first year of life," says Dr Jaroslav Koch, who has them doing press-ups at six weeks old, and teaches them to climb ladders as soon as they can crawl, and to move along a horizontal beam without falling off. Yes, well, the trouble is, Dr Koch, that I believe you, absolutely. Do you remember the Teach Your Baby to Read System? We were all doing it 10 years ago, with our first babies. But nobody ever has the time or lunatic enthusiasm to try out these things on second or subsequent children. It gave Our Baby its first taste of power and, goodness, how it corrupted. You'd hold up a white card with CAT on it in large red letters. "It says Cat," you'd say encouragingly. "Come on now, what's it say?" Your baby would look at it and go on trying to get her toes in her mouth. Or she might snatch it away from you and start chewing it. Then you'd try CUP and DOG and she'd still go on holding out on you, and finally, infuriated at having bred a half-wit, you'd thrust TONGUE under her nose and she'd give it a kind of casual glance and say tongue in an off-hand way and go on cramming her fist in her mouth.

All it taught us was that Our Baby could read all right, if she wanted to, but she was damned if she was going to bother.

Looking back a few years and remembering how I felt at the end of the day, when they were only small and weak and I was big and strong, and then imagining Dr Koch's infant Herculeses, flexing their tiny, milk-fed muscles at me and doing 50 press-ups before the 6 a.m. feed, fills me with sheer horror. I don't want them to be able to climb vertically up a ladder as soon as they can crawl, Dr Koch, or creep along the upstairs bannister without falling off. Life is full enough of excitement as it is. A baby only a few weeks old, he says impressively, will hang onto the mother's hair by the hands supporting its own weight. Yes, I know it will. That's one of the things I used to complain of.

It's a powerhouse we're sitting on, as it is, Dr Koch, don't you see that? People are only just beginning to realise the enormous potentiality, as yet unharnessed, that little children represent. A friend of mine, whose garage had three times failed to have her car ready for collection at the promised time, finally went to fetch it with two small children in tow, assured by a previous phone call that this time, honestly, it really would be finished. Of course it wasn't, so they allowed her to wait in their little shop, with the stands of sweets and crisps and spray-on polish and there she sat for 45 minutes until something snapped and, holding one child on her knee (a gesture less tolerant people might not have made), she allowed the other unsupervised carte blanche to wreak whatever havoc it liked. So simple, but so effective. For having unsuccessfully tried to restrain the child, they finally fell over themselves to produce the car while there was still a Smartie tube left intact.

Blue Peter knows it all; for years they've been subtly training children to be the most effective action group in the country. It all started off most laudably, getting them to collect scrap metal and postage stamps to build old people's homes and African schools. If United Dairies really do want their bottles back, all they have to do is to drop a word in

John Noakes's ear and the nation's doorsteps would be overflowing with empties the very next morning.

But the whole thing has taken a more sinister turn lately, with the spoons. You don't have to be paranoid to realise at once that Uri Geller is all part of a fiendish Red Plot, masterminded by the BBC and spearheaded by Blue Peter. I saw it in action, round the lunch table, only last week. They were arguing, Matthew and Dominic and Richard and Tristram, with the intensity that only six-year-olds can, about the basis of the Geller phenomena.

"He's got an electro-magnet," says Richard. "And he's got a vice in his pocket and he's got a laser-gun in his belt. And he's got cold hands to cool them down afterwards."

"He hasn't, he hasn't." Tristram and Matthew are passionate in their defence. "He just thinks about it, that's all; he thinks about it and that's all he needs to do."

Meanwhile, at the end of the table, Dominic is quietly rubbing away at his pudding-spoon, his knuckles white with effort. He puts it down on the table with a modest smile, its shank bent into a neat right angle. Tristram and Matthew are wildly triumphant. "There you are. That proves it. *Dominic* hasn't got a laser gun." Even Richard is impressed. I have to go away to answer the telephone just then, and when I come back they are all rubbing away with a common purpose and the table is littered with screwed-up tin-plate.

Now, bent spoons are a matter of small importance in the great scheme of things, but if ever I saw a wedge's thin end, this is it. One moment they're collecting old milk-bottle tops for blind dogs, the next they're snarling up all your cutlery. Where is it all going to end, I ask myself? Superbaby, with the strength of a commando and the inhibitions of a three-year-old, subtly seduced by subversive Sesame Street, and ready to overthrow society before his teeth are through.

16

Sackcloth and ashes

"It Was Not My Fault says Jimmy's Mum" was the disturbing headline I saw the day after Connors's defeat by Roscoe Tanner in the Wimbledon quarterfinals. Not my own newspaper, but one viewed across a crowded bus and the more interesting for that. I was tempted to edge my way further over towards it, to discover why Jimmy's mum felt it necessary to make this public statement disclaiming responsibility for her son's failure. The reason I didn't is that I have been wary about reading things in other people's newspapers since an incident some years ago when I had been unobtrusively (I thought) reading a Daily Express over its owner's shoulder and he, getting out at Cannon Street, had folded up the paper and handed it to me, with a polite but pointed bow.

Before I go any further, Mrs Connors, I would like to put on record that I don't think it was your fault either. I feel able to say this quite categorically, in spite of not having read the rest of the article and therefore not knowing whether you hadn't collected his tennis shoes from the menders, or made sure he got to bed early the night before, or merely, as mothers will, cheered a bit too loudly in the stands and put him off his stroke. Much the same sort of thing happened to my son's friend, John, in the School Sports Day First Year 50-yard sprint – halfway up the track he caught sight of his Dad standing on the sidelines pointing a camera at him and froze. In fact the lad went on to win, but if he hadn't I know whose fault it would have been. Or would have been said to have been. But I think I speak for the mothers of the nation – although of course I don't know about your nation, Mrs Connors, because I believe you have an altogether different attitude towards motherhood over there, living as you do in a matriarchal society where possibly more is expected of a mother – when I say that any chap old enough to reach the Wimbledon quarter-finals ought to be responsible for his own tennis shoes. It was not your fault, Mrs Connors. Absolutely not.

My own paper analysed Connors's game stroke by stroke but made no mention at all of his mother, or her possible contribution to his failure. This was disappointing but not surprising. It is a little-known fact that all Grauniad* compositors are members of a very strict Wesleyan sect and have taken an oath to guard the moral welfare of the rest of us, so far as is in their power, by refusing to handle stories of a frivolous, sensational, or salacious nature. This is why all Grauniad readers are socially disadvantaged, knowing nothing of scandal in high places, and why so many of us also subscribe to Private Eye.

Goodness knows, there are enough things of my own which I do, or don't do, which are clearly not my fault, without having to set about proving that things I've had nothing to do with aren't my fault either. When you really come to think about it, or at least when I really come to think about it, very few things are actually my fault. There are so many external factors operating in any situation that only a really determined martyr need go about beating her breast and crying *mea culpa*. There's always some convenient doorstep to deposit the burden of blame on – either the weather's too hot or the Hoover's not working or the shops were shut or it was a printer's error. As my daughter said, coming second by a fingernail in the breaststroke at the Girl Guides' Swimming Gala, "It wasn't my fault – the girl who won had very long arms."

People have been going on about environment, and its influence on little children, for far too long, and this is the sort of thing it leads to. Give them all the environment in the world and they'll still go and make a mess of things. Mrs Connors's son, Jimmy, is the living proof of that. I prefer to put the blame squarely on hereditary factors myself. You may have noticed that there isn't a single spelling mistake in this article. This isn't because of careful sub-editing. It's because I'm an exceedingly good speller. Now my husband, on the other hand, is an appalling speller. A friend once asked him to sign the back of a passport photo for him with his name and occupation, because he didn't know any vicars. A few days later a suspicious Passport Office official rang up the hospital to say was there actually a Dr Peter Fenwick and did he really work there? Oh yes, said his secretary, why? Because, said the man from the Passport Office, they found it hard to believe in a doctor who couldn't spell Medical Practitioner. That's him, said my husband's secretary.

Whenever the children move into a different class at school I think it's only fair to explain to their teachers about this poor-spelling gene that they've inherited. From the other side of the family, of course – it's not my fault.

During the 1960s, in the days of hot-metal printing, the Guardian was published in Manchester and had to be transported quickly to London before it could be copy-edited properly. In those days the number of typos that could be spotted in any edition of the Guardian earned it the nickname of the Grauniad, given to it by Private Eye.

TRIVIAL PURSUITS

17

Come fly with me

Two thousand feet up above the Romney marshes is no place for anybody with a poor head for heights and no sense of direction. I can easily become disorientated, even on the ground, surrounded by landmarks and able to switch off the engine and take stock, consulting the map and working out, after some thought, which way lies left and which right, to gaze at the sun and consider at my leisure whether I am heading east or west and whether it is a desirable direction. But the aeroplane has only one engine and it is inadvisable, at my level of proficiency, to switch it off. One engine has always seemed plenty down at sea level but up here it feels a bit inadequate. The compass is no help. It reads north but I have no idea where it is that I am north of. Actually, flying an aeroplane is not too difficult at all. It is the ancillary skills that are so hard to come by – finding one's way and understanding the man in the control tower at the other end of the intercom. His messages come through like machine-gun fire, rapid and incomprehensible and interspersed with crackle, but always with a sense of extreme urgency in no way disguised by the fact that he is apparently speaking Urdu. He may be telling me to get out of the way of a DC10 immediately, before I am mown down, or he may simply be advising me which runway to use. I wouldn't know. And actually, I can't see any runways at all. Once in the air the landscape fades into uniformity and the only things which I can identify with any certainty are Dungeness power station and the English Channel. If I can see either or both of these significant landmarks then I have a fair idea of where I am, give or take a mile or two in all directions. If I can't see either of them, then I'm lost.

This sounds serious but it's not really serious because I have Ellie beside me. Ellie is my instructor and the aeroplane is dual control on the whole, although only one set of brakes is working on my side. Sometimes we have very exciting landings because we forget until it's almost too late that only one of us has control of the brakes. But Ellie is a carefree girl and this doesn't seem to bother her particularly so I don't see that it's my place to worry about it. The brakes aren't the only things not working on Zulu Oscar. Zulu Oscar is the aeroplane. She has seen better days. There are many, many dials in front of me but I don't have to bother about some of them because they have labels stuck on them saying NOT IN USE. There's another notice stuck to the control panel which says THIS AEROPLANE NOT LICENSED FOR AEROBATICS – but that is the least of my worries. Ellie is extremely fond of Zulu Oscar for all she sometimes refers to her as a clapped out old heap of scrap metal. Whenever we walk round her (on the ground, that is), she pats her where her rump would be if she were a horse. Every now and then she strokes her withers fondly and sometimes she picks up loose handfuls of fuselage to demonstrate how close she is to retirement. This can be very disconcerting.

Ellie cannot understand why I cannot see the runway. She explains to me exactly where it is, down there just by the big black hangar, out of my window and slightly to the left. I still can't see it but of course I pretend I can, because I feel so foolish otherwise. I never actually do see it until we are hovering about fifteen feet above the tarmac but I have learned to suppress my pleased gasp of recognition at this point, or Ellie gives me a funny look and I know she knows I haven't really seen it at all before, not until this very moment.

I am at a distinct advantage having Ellie for an instructor, because Ellie is a feminist and has this theory, which she is ever anxious to substantiate, that women make better pilots than men. They are lighter on the controls, she says. Certainly, I am very light on the controls indeed, because I have a horror of inducing any sudden unexpected movements in the aircraft. So I touch the controls as little as possible and make adjustments that could only be detected by a micrometer screw gauge and Ellie attributes this to delicacy of handling and not cowardice, which is nice.

Sometimes I think it's all a terrible mistake that I'm up here at all, because profound thoughts like these do tend to flit in and out of your mind when you're two thousand feet up trying to keep your wing tips level, like a man walking a tightrope across Niagara, balancing a pole. Down there in the clubhouse, before my first lesson, I was just about to call the whole thing off when another member came across and slapped me on the back. "Is this your wife's first lesson?" he asked my husband. "I wish mine would learn but I can't persuade her." My husband beamed with pride at his reluctantly adventurous wife and one of the children began to cry. "I don't want mummy to die," she said. She has an overdeveloped sense of drama. "Good heavens, don't be so silly," I said snappily. "I'm not going to die. I'm just going to learn to fly, that's all. Like daddy. Why, it's safer than driving a car." So they all say, but I think that's one of those statistics you can prove anything with. The other children had no sense of impending doom. They were taken up with examining the squadrons of model aeroplanes dangling from the roof. Sebastian makes them. Sebastian owns the club. He wears double-breasted suits and drives a pearl grey Aston Martin, which, if you are unwary enough to admire it, he will show you round in some detail. After he left the air force he got fed up with receiving mysterious telephone calls from African revolutionaries wanting him to fly MiGs as a mercenary pilot, so he started the club instead. After we have gone tamely home with the children on a Saturday night they have great games in the clubhouse, with pitched water-pistol battles. Sometimes children are a great blessing.

The last time we went down to the club poor Zulu Oscar was sitting in front of the clubhouse with no front wheel and her nose resting on a pile of old tyres. Someone had made an unfortunate landing in her and it had been decided to release her from active service and use her for spares. It was nothing but a relief to me but Ellie was sad. She did her first solo in Zulu Oscar and has a deep sentimental attachment to her. We go up in a plane called Whisky Echo now, which has brakes on both sides and a heater as well. I don't think I shall ever go solo, though. If God had meant me to fly, I sometimes tell myself, He'd have given me an airspeed indicator. Or at least a better sense of direction.

18

Vox Humana

There is a professor of neurophysiology in the South of France who collects shrunken heads. I know this is true because we saw them at a post-conference party one year – I believe he has a colleague in London who gets most of them for him at Sothebys. And, in case anyone should consider it unmannerly to accept a man's hospitality and then comment on his shrunken heads, I must add that it was a magnificent party, to which the discovery of the heads, nestling among the Louis Seize furniture, added only a final frisson of delight.

I mention this only to emphasise that other people besides my husband have peculiar hobbies.

My next husband (Punch once ran a series on this, or naturally the idea would never have occurred to me) – my next husband will collect postage stamps, or press wild flowers, or possibly breed mice, or almost anything else so long as it can be fitted into a space of about two or three cubic feet. What he will not do is collect harmoniums. Or American organs. (There is a fairly subtle difference between the two, depending on which way the air is drawn through the reeds, which those of you who are interested in them will know about and those who aren't, won't care about.) I would just like to make quite sure that no confusion exists in anyone's mind about the difference between the harmonium, or American organ, and the harmonica, or mouth organ. The latter is a small, totally inoffensive instrument, which can be slipped unobtrusively into anyone's breast pocket, while the former is rather bulkier than an upright piano, with stops, and foot pumps, and knee operated swells. It should ideally be situated in a chapel in the valley, surrounded by a crowd of lusty, hymn-singing Welshmen, and, wherever it is, one is enough. We had three at one time, all playing in slightly different keys. "Please don't let daddy buy another organ," the children plead when the car automatically slows down as we pass another derelict-looking chapel (we keep them in the playroom and they get a bit embarrassed when their friends come to tea ("Why does your dad need all those pianos?").

In fact the harmoniums don't really bother me anymore. You get used to anything, after a time. What does worry me is this correspondence he's carrying on with the gentleman at the Redundant Churches Fund, in St Andrew-by-the-Wardrobe, EC4 (with facts like this, who needs fiction?).

"Dear Dr Fenwick," he writes, "I'm pleased to be able to tell you that we have available a redundant Victorian organ of the kind you require, with a height of 16 feet . . ." My husband wrote back regretfully, explaining that the playroom is only 12 feet high, but only after a lot of thought. I know he is wondering about the structural soundness of knocking a hole through the playroom ceiling, and it is useless for me to protest that I do not wish to share a bedroom with the top end of a 16-foot diapason. He would only point out, quite reasonably, that there is nowhere else it could possibly go. "I am checking with the diocese," replies Mr St Andrew-by-the-Wardrobe, "to see whether the second organ I have in mind is a more manageable size." Please, St Andrew, please let it be enormously, definitively huge. Let it not be a mere

12 foot 6 inches, when he might very well, by some master feat of engineering, manoeuvre it through the playroom window, having first removed the frame, and make minor excavations in the ceiling to accommodate its pipes. "It's not actually right in the bedroom," he'd explain, "only just reverberating a little among the joists."

I am not on such strong ground as I used to be, however, when it comes to protesting about harmoniums. Not since I bought the pew. Fifteen feet of solid elm for £3, when they demolished the Methodist Church down the road. Half a dozen boy scouts delivered it one evening when we were out, and our baby-sitter very wisely kept the chain on the door and refused to let it in. So they left one end up against the front door, and when we got home pedestrians were tripping over the other. We got it in somehow, with about two feet of clearance either end of the hall, so that it was quite possible, by pushing one end hard up against the kitchen door, to open the front door, and vice versa. Then we realised that it might have been more convenient had the seat not been facing the staircase and the back obtruding into the hall. But it would have needed planning permission to turn it round, so we left it that way for a couple of months until we had a friend with a sharp saw coming to lunch one Sunday. (Since then we've had one 10-foot pew and one 5-foot one, which is much more manageable.) He arrived as we were carrying it out of the front door again, so that it could be bisected in the garden. There was a lot of scaffolding around the house just then; we were having a chimneystack repaired.

"Ah," he said, "I see you're taking the whole place down and putting up a church."

Which is probably the only possible solution.

19

Xmas party game

~

I don't think we'll be dabbling in the Occult again this year. It is not conducive to the Christmas spirit. At the time, in the rosy, post-prandial, port-ridden glow of a Boxing evening, a bit of table-tapping seemed an entertaining thought, and also an easy way of occupying the boys (like Donald Duck, my husband has three nephews) until we could decently pack them off to bed.

We conjured up Uncle Arthur pretty quickly. As relatives go, he seemed pretty good value, though there were initial difficulties in communication on account of his spelling – we were using a set of Scrabble letters and amazingly enough when you think that the average set of Scrabble letters spells uuiofa, Uncle Arthur's words were usually a bit short on vowels.

We established quite soon that he came from Morpeth, or Mpth as he economically put it, where he had some sort of smallholding or shpramf– sheep farming is fairly common in that part of Northumberland. A man of simple country tastes, he admitted a fondness for cleaks, which might well have been cakes and ale unless it was a form of

87

Northumbrian clog dance. Alas, he was called up in 1914, fought at the battle of Mons, and died gallantly for his country in Brussels, according to Uncle Hugh, a romantic at heart, or drunkenly in a Munich beer cellar, according to Uncle Peter, or of a Christmas surfeit of brussels sprouts according to the nephews. Burless was the word he actually used. It could have been brucellosis I suppose. We never thought of that.

Uncle Arthur was a bit coy about his sex life. In his glass tumbler persona he shuffled indecisively about the board, displaying an out-dated reticence even on such innocuous matters as his wife's name. "Estril" was all we could get out of him. Hester Eileen, said my sister-in-law, somewhat improbably, but it seemed fairly evident to me, as I explained to the boys, that what he was trying to tell us, in a delicate, Edwardian way, was that he had an *erstwhile* wife. We thought at the time that he'd just gone off her, that his joining up in 1914 was escapism rather than patriotism, but now, 12 months later and completely sober, I can see that we did the old boy an injustice. It is obvious now that she too was carried off by the brucellosis. And that the shrampf was not a sheep farm at all, but Uncle Arthur's spiritual shorthand way of indicating a farm with a cowshed, which would naturally explain the brucellosis. Picture the scene in all its poignancy. Christmas 1917, and Uncle Arthur with a few days leave trudging through the blizzard across the lonely Mpth moors to his shpramf, tended in his absence by the faithful Hester. Straight to the shippon or cowshed he goes, for it is milking time. But Hester's milking stool is empty; she lies upstairs, feverish and fading fast, and Arthur, sobbing, clasps her in his arms for a last farewell. And then once she is erstwhile, he staggers bravely back to the trenches, the dreaded Brucella already coursing through his veins.

The nephews were practically quacking with excitement by this time but getting a bit impatient with Uncle Arthur's dickie spelling. We added Yes and No cards to the corners of the board and found that by presenting him with a multiple choice questionnaire the information transfer was speeded up a lot. The old fellow appreciated this and fairly darted about the table, answering questions as fast as we could fire them. Yes, the war in Vietnam would end by next Christmas, Yes it would snow by New Year's Eve, and Yes, the youngest nephew's school report was totally unfair. No, Uncle Hugh would not open another bottle of port that evening. Soon he was making wild and grandiose promises, to materialise at the top of the Christmas tree at midnight, to fetch Aunt Hester along tomorrow night, to guarantee that Arsenal would win the cup. The adults, one by one, retired to their port, leaving Uncle Arthur, indefatigable, and the nephews, over-excited, to carry on. The trouble started when Uncle Arthur, for no apparent reason, suddenly switched his allegiance and declared that Chelsea would win the cup and furthermore, that Arsenal stank.

It was about this time that the youngest nephew began to suspect that someone, somewhere, was taking the mickey out of somebody.

He glared round the table at his older brothers. "Uncle Arthur," he asked, in horrified tones, "Is anybody cheating?" Uncle Arthur prevaricated for a while, but eventually sidled over to the Yes card. "Is it Simon?" demanded the youngest nephew. "No," "Is it Neil?" "No". Quick as a flash his brothers chorused, "Is it Mark, Uncle Arthur?" Without a moment's hesitation the tumbler shot over to the other side of the board.

With a howl of rage the youngest nephew rose to his feet. "You're a dirty great liar, Uncle Arthur," he shrieked and swept the tumbler off the table.

It took quite a time to calm him down. No wonder none of us had heard of Uncle Arthur. He was obviously the blkshp. of the family. Anyway, there shouldn't be any trouble this Christmas. The nephews are old enough to learn a nice, gentlemanly game like strip poker.

20

Putting a spoke in it

⌒

It is quite possible, given the kind of reckless optimism that makes men set off across the Atlantic in rowing boats, to get most of the way down Herne Hill with one's brakes off. The temptation, when rounding the last bend, to decelerate by dragging my feet, thus scuffing the toes of my shoes like mother told me not to, is still almost irresistible. But I've achieved a fair degree of abandonment now, and if the lights are green at the bottom I can even remove a hand, the left one usually, momentarily from the handlebars to signal my intention to go to the bank. Coming back up the hill I outstrip myself each time. There is little doubt in my mind that by Christmas – and if I could get the bike into first gear – I could make it to the red patch on the pavement quite near the house where I dropped a can of paint eight years ago.

That's my daughter's bike, the one with the dodgy first gear. My bike has no gears at all. Come to that, my bike has no spokes in the wheels either, which is a more fundamental problem. In a world that contains Concorde and the Sistine chapel and the theory of relativity, it is easy to overlook man's simpler achievements. Stop for a moment, get off your bike and marvel at the intricacies of spoking that go on in your wheels.

I expect you thought it was all machine-made, or computer-programmed, but it's not. Every one of those spokes (thirty-six of them in most cases, although mine has thirty-two on the front and forty on the back, which makes working out the pattern even more difficult) was put in by hand and fixed at the end with a little hollow screw and tightened just the right amount so that the axle ends up in the middle and the whole wheel spins true. Penelope could have spent seven years weaving bicycle wheels, easily, and hardly noticed that Odysseus was gone.

It was not so much the energy crisis that underlined my need for a bike of my own, as a spell of enforced car deprivation, initially for reasons which loyalty to the driver forbids me to enter into too deeply here, and subsequently because the car is suffering from iatrogenic disease brought on by garage mechanics.

The first thing you notice about not having a car is the time you save by not collecting jumble, not taking the children swimming, not driving down into Kent to pick strawberries, and not going out to dinner with anyone living more than ten minutes off the 68 bus route. The hours not spent, from five until eight, three evenings a week, not watching cricket. But that was until the heady day when my son batted number two and scored 19 not out against All Souls Junior Mixed, Peckham, and I wasn't there to see it. Then the thought of my son and his friends, with their green-kneed white flannels and their Walter Mitty expectations of every innings, so moved me that I sought alternative means of transport, and leaped onto my daughter's bike each evening to join the other maternal cricketing groupies around the boundary, staked out in the park with such objects as a few little flags and a park bench or two and Mr Henry's floppy white umpire's hat which, with the awful weather we had all the way through the cricket season, he hardly ever needed to keep the sun out of his eyes. It was too late, of course, because by then the lad had passed his cricketing peak and slid slowly down the batting order for the rest of the summer.

When I last cycled – in Cambridge, twenty years ago – there was not the same competition for road space that one finds now in Inner London. I suppose there were cars on the roads even then, but I do not remember that they counted for much. We swarmed over the road, two, or three, or four abreast and made no concessions to motorised transport. But, after years of driving, I find it hard to rediscover a bicycling identity.

Sometimes I feel as though I'm a car and have to squash the urge to make competitive getaways at traffic lights with the knowledge that I'm not in the running any more. Sometimes I feel like a pedestrian and get off and wheel it across while the lights are red, which is quicker anyway. Sometimes I think I'm invisible, when pedestrians step right into the gutter, which is my patch, and hover indecisively there waiting for a traffic opening, leaping back indignantly when I run over their toes.

In India, like Cambridge, everybody cycles, ignoring cows and water buffaloes and any form of highway code; and it was this that so filled me with nostalgia that I bought my own bike there, a couple of weeks ago, from the Rand Bicycle and Rickshaw Company, Allahabad. In my opinion it was, at £18, an extremely good buy, even with no spokes in its wheels. Mr Desai would have spoked it for me, had I so wished; but he thought – we both thought – that it might travel better without, airline officials being what they are and not noted for their delicate handling of other people's property, no matter how largely writ the Fragile label on it. So he took my bicycle to bits and tied the spokes together and put the ball bearings in paper bags and wrapped the whole thing up in a canvas cocoon sewn around with twine, so that it could truthfully be described as a package, rather than a bicycle, so fulfilling the conditions under which Indian Airlines were prepared to transport it.

There were people out there, intelligent, responsible people, who maintained that it would not be possible to buy a bicycle in Allahabad and carry it back to Heathrow via Benares, Delhi and the Taj Mahal without running into trouble and officiousness at some airport desk or another. And yet here it is, sitting in the dining room at Herne Hill with all the other family bikes; in pieces, yes; spokeless, certainly. There are people who maintain that I'll never get it back together again. But compared to the vicissitudes of its journey here, that doesn't seem to me to be an insuperable problem. If everyone would just go away and leave me alone for seven years, I'm sure I could solve it.

21

Unfair competition

~

It is disconcerting to find oneself, unwittingly, in the forefront of a trend. Now that Clement Freud is playing it on the QE2, and Omar Sharif is teaching it in the Sunday Times, and Queen Margrethe is seen having a friendly game with her husband in the Radio Times, and no colour supplement is complete without its Special Offer Backgammon Board, there should be some satisfaction in remembering that I learnt the game years ago, at my mother-in-law's knee, to curry favour. She wasn't actually my mother-in-law then, but I had hopes of her. I was staying with her at the time in her house near Nairobi and I felt I had lost a certain amount of ground over the spiders on the bathroom wall. They looked to me very like tarantulas but she said they kept the mosquitoes down and refused to do anything about them. For a month I bathed standing up, maintaining a constant vigilance. It wasn't too bad when you could see where they were but take your eyes off them for a second and they would disappear, scuttling behind the pictures, or the towel rail, or into your nightdress, so that every garment had to be picked up with extreme caution, at arm's length, between finger and thumb, as though it had been dipped in prussic acid.

So, ingratiatingly, hoping to recover the face I had lost over the spiders, I allowed her to teach me backgammon and, by the end of the holiday, had become as addicted as she was herself. It was a passion that reached its zenith during my first pregnancy and I took a board into hospital with me to while away the visiting hours. The first time we played when we were back in the ward, our daughter safely delivered, the girl in the next bed sat up and said, "My God, so that was it." She had apparently been in the labour ward next to mine, where we had had a few long-drawn out games between contractions and, hearing the staccato snap and crackle of the dice and counters had, in a pethidine-induced haze, received the impression that the General Lying-In Hospital was under heavy machine gun fire.

Since then we haven't played much but, hearing that the first British Backgammon Amateur Championships were to be held this year, it was tempting to try our luck. An entrance fee of £2 each seemed a reasonable enough price to pay for a night out at the Hilton, where the London heats were being held, with coffee and biscuits thrown in.

The Hilton ballroom, all red carpets and crystal chandeliers, with vast collages around the walls executed by some giantess with a crude eye for colour, had a hundred backgammon boards. In the centre of the room was a dais, occupied by two beautiful girls, an Expert and a Master of Ceremonies. The role of the beautiful girls was to shake the dice, alternately, and so eliminate to some extent the element of chance. The role of the Expert was to act as adjudicator, because a great many of the competitors had also played the game almost exclusively with their mothers-in-law and not everybody's house rules bore a strong relationship to the official version of the game. The Master of Ceremonies had a hard time of it on the whole. His principal responsibility was to call out each throw, which wasn't as easy as it sounds because some of the competitors had evidently learned the game the night before and were continually three moves behind. After each game he had to move the hundred White players, on the outer perimeter, one place round in a counter clockwise direction. This had all the grace and charm of a barn dance and allowed plenty of time to establish a pleasant relationship with one's opponent before the next game began, because at every progression somebody's nerve cracked and the MC had to dart about matching up people whose opposite numbers had disappeared. He was very patient about all this.

The British must make the best amateurs in the world. So gentlemanly we were, so quick to congratulate our opponents on a good move, to commiserate with them on an unlucky throw, to make little regretful placatory gestures if we happened to take one of their men off, to say at the end of each match, win or lose, what a splendid game it had been and how much we were enjoying the evening. All this was so until the final match, when I had as my opponent a chap who wanted to win. He was not, naturally enough, British, and in fact I wouldn't dream of disclosing his nationality, although I daresay wild horses might drag it out of me. He wanted to win because he reckoned, if he got the maximum eight points for this last game, he would qualify for the national finals in July. Not only did he want to win but he was undoubtedly better than I was and gave the impression of a man who spent most of his twilight hours at Crockfords. When I asked him how he was doing, he said very well indeed, with no self-deprecation at all. He moved his counters rapidly, aggressively, and he was the only person I had met that evening who didn't seem to be enjoying himself. Between each move he sent his attendant blonde nymph around the neighbouring tables to see how everyone else was doing, or over to the score board pinned on the wall behind us to check on his position in the league.

All this unnerved me so completely that my game disintegrated quickly and he was soon in an impregnable position and had doubled me, so that a win would give him four points. But this, according to his reckoning, was not enough and there came a moment some moves later when he leaned across the board and made a most improper suggestion. I was, he said, for he had sent the nymph to check on my score too, not in the running for the finals. So if I were to offer him a redouble now it would not affect my own chances and would give him eight points if he won, happily consolidating his position. What about it? This was something like asking the last horse in the National to bet on himself when the first is already within sight of the winning post, a move either suicidal or of supreme over-confidence. A frisson of disapproval at this blatant attempt to cheat ran round the adjacent table where Red, in my position, had long since demolished his opponent and they swivelled their chairs round to see what was going on.

It was a difficult position for the genuine British amateur to find herself in. Obviously one could not sneak. Besides, it seemed to me that the only disadvantage I was likely to be able to put him under was a moral one, so I might as well make the most of it. So I redoubled, like he wanted.

Now the fascinating thing about backgammon, which puts it, to my mind, head and shoulders above ludo or snakes and ladders, is the amazing twists of fortune, which come when you least expect them, or deserve them. We were within a few moves of the end of the game – because to save time the games were not played out to completion but limited to 44 moves – when I was able to remove one of his men from the board. It is true that this took, under the circumstances, a good deal of courage. I found myself wondering whether he might produce a revolver from his velvet smoking jacket and shoot one of us and, if so, which. A man off the board at the end of the game would score very heavily against him and I could see from his pallor and the way he wiped his palms on his trousers that at last there was more adrenaline coursing through his veins than through my own. He hated the next few minutes but I was feeling quite relaxed by then and with one or two more lucky throws

I was in a much better position when the whistle blew. The tournament scoring system was complicated and the people at the next table added up several times, just to make sure. He won in the end but it was only a minor four-point victory and seemed to give him little satisfaction.

But it's worrying to think that the game plumbed such unimaginable depths of depravity in my own character. Quite apart from the sadistic streak that relished every bead of sweat upon his forehead, I actually found myself wanting to win. It's almost enough to make one lose one's amateur status.

POLITICAL PITFALLS

22

Playing the party game

~

If the omens and portents are correct, and there is a
General Election this year, I think I should like to make
it quite clear now, so that there will be no hurt feelings
nearer the date, that we shall not be holding an Election
party this time. There's no reason why we should, except
the awkward precedent that one or other or both of us
has had one every General Election since 1957, but really
it's a rotten idea. I can't think why we ever started it.

It was a beautiful June night, the last one, and there we
were, all excited, with coloured lights (red and blue) in the
apple tree, and a lovely chart stretching from one end of
the political spectrum to the other, with little coloured flags
(pink and red and light blue and dark blue) with everyone's
names written on them, and splendid cartoons drawn by a
friend of a few of the leading political figures of the day,– I

can't remember now who they were, but never mind. And some sort of wine cup with dry ice in it to make it fizz. And food. All the ingredients, you might think, of a pretty good do, and so it was to begin with. It was some time before we realised that all was not as merry as it might be. Some people didn't like the colour of the flag we'd allotted to them – it's amazing how touchy people can be if you misjudge their shade of political opinion.

Parties are peculiar affairs anyway, with all your friends gathered together, instead of meeting each other in carefully pre-selected groups. We liked them all, motley crowd though they were, but we weren't at all sure that they liked each other. MPs keep up a fiction that away from the Chamber and in the bar they are all the best of backslapping chums, but I don't believe a word of it. Not after that party. By about 1.30 a.m., when the results were beginning to flow in and the television computers were wildly analysing trends, the party had polarized completely, left-wingers alcoholically morose round the home set in the sitting-room, right-wingers drunkenly jubilant round the hired one in the playroom. That's when the truth struck us, and we stood in the hall looking at each other and we realised that all these people actually cared. They thought it mattered. Everybody but us believed that the election of the government of their choice would herald a bright new political and economic dawn. The system being what it is, they couldn't all be right, as it is unlikely that any election will end in a draw, so, whatever the result, half our friends were doomed to end the evening downcast and dejected, and that's no way for your guests to leave a party.

It's sad that I feel this way, because I would love to be politically committed again. Of all the games people play, politics can be the most fun, and elections the most exhilarating. When I was twelve I was tremendously political. I was a member of the Vermin Club, which was founded as a rude gesture by the Tories after Aneurin Bevan had referred to them as lower than vermin. If you enrolled a dozen more members you became a Chief Stoat, or a King Rat or something, and had a white badge instead of a blue one. I became a Chief Stoat in no time at all. It wasn't difficult at Cheltenham Ladies College. In the holidays I addressed envelopes and pushed them through letterboxes and canvassed for my father, who became the first Tory Mayor in the history of our town, known locally as Little Moscow. His election after his year in office ended in a draw, so he tossed a coin for it and lost.

They don't have cliffhangers like that nowadays. It all made very fine copy for the local newspaper and they used it for years, every time they had cause to refer to a member of the family. When I was married, years later, it was "Daughter of Mayor Who Lost Seat on Spin of Coin Weds Doctor". When my brother qualified it was "Son of Mayor Who Lost... etc... etc". I daresay in a decade or so they'll dig it out again, "Grandson of Mayor who Lost Seat on Toss of Coin Goes to Pot".

But ever since those days, my political beliefs have swung uncertainly between the influences of environment and heredity. I suppose I must be the only Labour-voting, paid-up member of the South Norwood Conservative Party. How can this have come about, I daresay some of you are asking, as indeed I do myself? Well, basically it's because every time anyone knocks on the door in the evening and wants to know if we'll join, my husband says, "ah, it's my wife you want to see," and disappears. I don't blame him for this, because I do it myself if Jehovah's Witnesses call during the day. "You'd better come back later," I say, twisting a corner of my apron if I happen to be wearing one, and attempting to drop my lower jaw a little and possibly salivate at the edges; "he'll see you then". They never do. It seems to be part of a system of role allocation we've worked out unconsciously.

So, there I am, left with these two nice people on the doorstep – they always travel in pairs because they don't like to send their ladies out alone after dark in South Norwood – and the difficult thing is that they somehow assume from the start that I am one of Them. This annoys me, because I like to think that I have cast off the shackles of heredity and achieved a kind of classlessness, that nobody, at a mere glance, can slot me into any political pigeon-hole. On the other hand, I don't wish to make an issue of it because, who knows, they may well be right. I don't know – I haven't made up my mind yet. Anyway, if I refused they might expect me to be able to defend another set of principles that I don't really believe in wholeheartedly either. So I join, and then when the Labour Party comes round I am able to say, well, I can't actually join you. But maybe I might vote for you.

Things get more complicated still on polling day. As I go into the polling station there are several ladies standing around outside, with vast coloured rosettes in their buttonholes. Most of them I know by sight. One or two I am on coffee-drinking terms with. I may well have indicated to more than one of them that there is a fairly strong probability that their party will get my vote and, indeed, at the time I am sure I meant it. Now I slope past them uneasily, giving a shifty smile to both right and left. As I come out again I have to run the gauntlet of several pairs of outstretched hands. They want me to give them my polling card, as a mediaeval lady might toss a favour to the knight of her choice. I make little, regretful, patting gestures at my pockets, hoping to indicate to them all that I have most unfortunately left my card at home on the kitchen mantlepiece, but if any of them cares to call round for it later in the day, why, I'll be delighted to hand it over.

But the whole thing bothers me because without a measure of pure political faith, how can anybody with only a media acquaintanceship with the principals and principles involved vote with any degree of conviction? If you want my opinion (though if I were you I wouldn't touch it with a barge-pole as my opinions are tatty, second-rate affairs, entirely dependent on who has been talking to in the last ten minutes), anyway, if you do want my opinion it is that all the politicians who one knows personally, are decent, likeable, high-principled chaps, just like you and me. All the rest are unscrupulous seekers after self-aggrandisement, except for Roy Jenkins and Robert Carr, who are soft options. Everybody likes them.

So the next election we'll spend by ourselves round the television, enjoying whatever happens without having to apologise to anyone. With a bottle of sparkling Vouvray perhaps – no election merits real champagne. Anyone who feels the same way as we do is welcome to join us, and the rest of you can go and work yourselves up somewhere else. Whoever wins, I shall be just as happy. Or just as sad.

23

Ted and Margaret and various other elections

~

One thing that really puts me off from becoming leader of the Conservative party, is the thought of having to go through all those elections. Elections can give rise to such a lot of unpleasantness. You must have to want to be leader a lot more than I do, voluntarily to subject yourself to the possibility of three in a row.

I think I was very traumatised by elections when I became a school prefect. Prefects at my school emerged by a reasonable blend of magic circle and democracy, whereby the upper school made nominations, which were then gone over by headmistress and staff to remove any obvious undesirables or anarchic elements, producing a final list on which we voted. This method had worked very well since the school's foundation and there seemed no reason why it should not continue in perpetuity. It varied not at all except for the term I was elected, when there was no election. What happened instead was this.

On the day which should have been election day, our headmistress, instead of giving us the lecture on electoral responsibility and the moral necessity for using one's vote

wisely, which was her wont on these occasions, told us instead
that there would be no election after all, because there were
only two vacancies and only two girls on the nomination list
were considered to be worthy of the rank of prefect. These
were myself and a girl called Jennifer Buckingham-Pallis.
That's not her real name. I am not going to tell you her
real name, although I remember it perfectly well. I think it
as well to draw a thin shroud of anonymity over the whole
disgraceful affair. Not because I think it might involve the
editor in a libel suit, although of course I am always mindful
of that possibility, but because my old school has, in the past,
proved itself over-sensitive to criticism. A much older and
more distinguished Old Girl than I, was, so we were always
told, thrown out of the Old Girls' Guild for publishing a
novel in which the school, only lightly disguised, appeared
in a poor light. And although we are quite happy with the
state system of education, we do have two daughters and I
do like to keep my options all open, even if I hope never
to have to take them up. Also, I do not wish to be unfair
to Jennifer Buckingham-Pallis. It was not really her fault.

Well, as you can imagine, our headmistress's
announcement produced certain stirrings of unrest, not
unlike those generated in the Conservative party some years
ago at the election of Sir Alec Douglas-Home. Everybody
knew, or thought they knew, the reason for this curious
non-election. Our headmistress was well known to have an
eye for the illustrious, and Jennifer Buckingham-Pallis's
father was somebody pretty important, like governor of
the Bank of England or a cabinet minister or something.
It was apparent to us all that, in order to get in good with
Mr Buckingham-Pallis (or Lord Buckingham-Pallis, or
General Sir Laurence Buckingham-Pallis or Lord Chief
Justice Buckingham-Pallis or whatever he was) she had fixed
Jennifer's election, with me thrown in to make the whole
thing less suspicious.

I was pretty annoyed about it all but I suppose it must,
– although I didn't give a lot of thought to this at the time

– have been a good deal worse for Jennifer Buckingham-Pallis. Nobody, after all, suggested that I had only been elected because of my father who, although a very fine man indeed, and well liked in our own small corner of north-east Lancashire, was not really illustrious. Not on a national scale. Not like Jennifer Buckingham-Pallis's father. All the same, it was some time before I could wear my prefect's badge with confidence along the marble corridors of power and it gave me a deep understanding of Sir Alec and how he must have felt. No wonder he went about the Palace of Westminster grinding his teeth and muttering, "All right, if they want an election then, by Jove, they'll get one."

After this I had nothing much to do with elections for some time, until our eldest child was about three and I enrolled her at the local playgroup. We had only just moved into the area and I wasn't yet on familiar terms with anyone except Phyllis in the dairy, who later ran off with the egg man, which is another story and even more likely to be libellous. So I was quite surprised, one day when I was going into the playgroup pushing a pushchair with a baby in it and hung about with various small children, to be approached by a girl pushing a baby in a pushchair and similarly encumbered with other little clutching hands, who said the playgroup annual general meeting was next week and how would I like to be secretary? I am always pleased when anyone thinks me capable of doing anything, and, as I hadn't learned then that the only qualification necessary for serving on the committee of any voluntary body is a willingness to say yes when asked (or an inability to say no), I felt gratified and agreed. "But," I warned her, "nobody knows me, you know. I probably won't get elected." "That's no problem," she said, taking one hand off the pushchair to wave it about in airy dismissal of what I couldn't help feeling was an important issue, "we'll take care of that." And indeed they did, for on election night I was voted into office by several people whom I didn't know from Adam. The following day I went along to take coffee with the new chairman. "Well," I said, "that all went very smoothly last night." "It certainly didn't," she said. "Didn't you realise that all the wrong people got elected? I mean, except us? Mrs Andrews and Mrs Bates were so determined to get on they must have been lobbying." "Oh," I said, "oh dear. But I daresay they'll be all right. Anyway, there's nothing we can do about it now." "Oh yes there is," said the chairman. "We can co-opt the others on."

So that's what we did and we had rather a large committee for the rest of the year with all the right people on it. Mrs Andrews and Mrs Bates were a bit of a drag though. I found the whole episode very instructive and rewarding and was charmed by the idea of being able to co-opt the right people onto committees if you couldn't get them elected by simple democratic means. Thereafter, whenever I have found myself in charge of any committee, I have nearly always managed to avoid any actual voting at elections – which can be a distasteful procedure arousing bad feeling – by trying to ensure that the number of candidates and the number of vacancies are the same and, if the former exceed the latter, then passing a quick resolution at the beginning of the meeting, adjusting the constitution to allow the surplus to be co-opted in some capacity. I can see that this form of committee management is open to criticism and is very like that practised by my former headmistress, but I think I do it is a bit more subtly.

I suppose, as far as the Tory party's concerned, that the principle of co-option might make for rather unwieldy leadership. Bulganin and Khrushchev seemed to work all right, but I daresay Thatcher and Whitelaw and Prior and Peyton and Howe would be going a bit too far.

24

Using the right wrong word

~

Some people attach a lot of importance to having the right tool for the job, but I think this shows a certain rigidity of character. You can get by pretty well most of the time with the wrong tool, provided it's the right wrong tool. You can, for example, scrape off old wallpaper fairly efficiently with a fish slice, but it's much more difficult to pick up fried eggs with a paint-stripper. It's something to do with the angle of the handle and the width of the blade, and whoever designs them might like to do a bit of re-thinking with fried eggs in mind.

Last Christmas we made a record of the infant school carol service, always a very touching occasion, and this involved a lot of tricky, split-second timing of each item while we were cutting the tape to the right length. My husband worked out quite a good method for doing this, which shows you the advantage of having a razor-edged scientific mind in the family. When he said, "Ready", I would put down my book and leave my comfortable armchair by the fireside and go into the cold, uncentrally heated hall and stand by the grandfather clock. When he said "Now" I would grab hold of the pendulum and stop it and read out the time on the clock to the nearest second. When he said "Go" I would give it a swing to get it going again and go back and pick up my book and sit down for a couple of minutes until he called out "Ready" again. When we were half way through the second side I said to him, "Don't you think it would be a good idea to borrow the headmaster's stopwatch like we did last year?" He looked surprised. "I don't see why," he said, "this works perfectly well."

You can usually get by with the wrong tool because most things are imprecise in function and interchangeable, so we start the car with a six-inch piece of wire when we lose the keys, and, if you want to find *Bartlett's Familiar Quotations*, it's holding up the shelf in the kitchen where the bracket has come off the wall. It's all right with things but it's not so easy with words. The right word for a particular job can make all the difference between a sluttish, slap-happy kind of sentence, the same sort of sentence as our kitchen shelf, and a satisfying piece of prose conveying a precise message to the listener.

During the February election campaign we saw a tele-recording of Enoch Powell addressing a meeting in his Martin-Luther-King-in-the-pulpit style. "Let us," he said with great deliberation, "tergiversate no longer." I think that's what he said, but it may have been "Let us have no more tergiversation," – with elections following swiftly on each other's heels these days one's memories easily become confused. Now, I had no more idea what he was talking about than the rest of his audience, who stirred, turning to each other with a little flurry of raised, inquiring eyebrows, but I had no doubt at all that it was the right word: a word chosen by an expert above all other words for its suitability and exactitude. We, of course, had an advantage over the audience in that we were sitting at home within easy reach of the *Concise Oxford Dictionary*, while they would almost certainly have forgotten it by the time they reached home and would have to spend the rest of the evening vainly leafing through the dictionary muttering tersiverate, terviscerate, and never discover that it means to turn one's back on oneself, turn one's coat, change one's party or principles, make conflicting statements. Or even (Chambers) to shuffle, shift, or use evasions. It seems to me that he's been doing a bit of tergiversating himself since then, but let that pass. There must be something to be said for a man who talks down to his audience so little that he can toss a word like that casually into their midst. Anyway, you can see what an excellent word it is. I stored it away in one of the many blank recesses of my mind, all ready to produce should the occasion arise, but I so seldom find myself engaged in a conversation of that level. The best I can do is to hang onto the letters TERSATE when I'm playing Scrabble, in the hope that my opponent, all unwittingly will put down GIVER, but I can see that it's a bit of an outside chance.

"While you're about it," I said to my husband while we were checking on tergiversate, "look up pragmatic." You may remember that Harold Wilson used to be very fond of pragmatic last time round. It was the *in word*, the magic talisman, in the way that social contract is now, and, although I sort of vaguely knew the kind of thing he meant by it, I thought perhaps I should look it up, just to make sure, in case we were in for another pragmatic government. "It means meddlesome," my husband said, "dogmatic, pedantic, officious, interfering with the affairs of others." Just the right word for the job, in fact, and I don't know why he's given it up in favour of social contract, unless perhaps he looked it up himself one day when he was trying to keep up with Enoch's vocabulary.

Elections produce a splendid crop of words, which may or may not be right for the job. On election night itself we settled down in front of the television set, ready for a bout of one of our favourite sports, which is mocking returning officers in the execution of their duty – just as mean as fox-hunting and a lot more fun – secure in the knowledge that the emotional climate and the pressure on all those wonderful men and their election machines to fill the next five or six hours with English as she is all too often spoke, would produce some memorable moments. Psephology was the word they were bandying about this year to send us all scuttling to our dictionaries, though I still don't know whether it's a study of the way people vote, or the way they tell opinion pollsters they are going to vote, and I'm not sure that Alastair Burnett does either.

Prize for the second-best wrong word for the evening went to the – victorious – Tory candidate who thanked all his party workers for their "unavailing help". I don't know though – everyone assumed he just pulled the wrong word out of the bag, but I have a feeling it was more of a Freudian slip. Someone down there in the shires hadn't been pulling his weight. But first prize, of a gold-plated, personalised, do-it-yourself, pocket swingometer, to the excited BBC commentator up in Huyton reporting Mr Wilson's appearance to address his constituents on some hastily erected platform. "Here he comes now," he burbled into his microphone, "up there on the scaffold … "

Not exactly the right word, but exactly the right wrong word.

I like to think that however unimaginable, indescribable a situation, somewhere the right word is waiting to describe it. While we were all glued to our various screens on January 6th 2021, watching the decline and fall of the American President, a friend emailed me the word of the day: 'sequaciousness' (17th century): 'the blinkered, unreasoning, and slavish following of another, no matter where it leads.'

NOBODY'S PERFECT

25

The art of the chiding letter

~

Whenever I feel jaded and put out by the frustrations of twentieth century life, I go and have a look at one of the most soothing exhibits in the British Museum. It's in the Third Egyptian Room, a peaceful place on the way to the mummies, and it is a letter, so the little card beneath it explains, written in 1210 BC by an Egyptian called Hori to another called Amenemope, chiding him for being unable to calculate the number of bricks needed to build a ramp 730 cubits long and 60 cubits high. I can't translate it word for word, because I can't read Egyptian hieroglyphics, but this hardly matters because it must be pretty similar in tone and content to the chiding letter we wrote to the man who was unable to calculate the number of tiles needed to cover our roof and ran out halfway through.

How comforting to realize that the Ancient Egyptians had these problems too. Do you suppose they sat around, those sloe-eyed, right-angled Egyptian ladies, on the steps of their pyramids or in their asses' milk baths, telling their friends, as we do, about the splendid little artisan they've found to do them a mosaic or knock them up a sphinx at the bottom of their garden?

"Of course, he's not cheap," I expect they said, "and he's not terribly good. But he's so nice to have around." And when you realize how long he's going to be around, brother, that counts, that counts.

But the point I want to make is that the letter Hori wrote to Amenemope was a chiding letter. Not an aggressive letter, or an abusive letter, or an outraged letter of high moral tone. Anyone can write those. The chiding letter is a whole art form, and has as its objective the achievement of results rather than the expression or release of pent-up feeling, so it lies at the opposite end of the letter-writing spectrum to the abusive letter, with the love letter falling somewhere about halfway between. Hori could have written quite a different sort of letter to Amenemope, and I daresay his wife was standing beside him urging him to do it, but it might not have got him his ramp built. I like to think that within minutes of getting that letter, Amenemope was round there at Hori's with another barrow-load of bricks.

Some people are notoriously bad at writing chiding letters. The man at the GMC who writes all those letters demanding back payment of subscriptions, for example, could do with a lighter touch. Phrases like "action is now being taken against" and "by December 10 at the latest" are quite out of place in a chiding letter. His whole approach is psychologically unsound anyway, based as it is on the premise that a series of demanding letters should become progressively more menacing, whereas of course the reverse is true. As the recipient's resistance hardens, the letters should become ever more persuasive and gently reproachful if it is to be overcome at all. It's not easy but then Art isn't easy.

Bank managers are terrible at writing chiding letters. It can be done – we have a delightful one from a Lloyds manager, requesting an interview to discuss an overdraft. It begins "I was amazed to discover it was ten months since our last pleasant meeting here – 1971 seems to have passed so quickly. I see that your facilities have been very fully used during the past 12 months, so perhaps we could meet again."

You see? On the other hand, my bank manager once wrote me a letter beginning "It has come to my notice" (a bad start, this, no chiding letter should ever start It has come to my notice or It has been drawn to my attention. The reader's hackles start to rise immediately.) "It has come to my notice," he said, "that a Dr Fenwick has again been using your National Westminster cheques to draw money on a Lloyds account." He went on in this vein for some time, complaining about the number of times he'd had to complain about this, and how it jammed up their computer. "Why don't you tell him," my bank manager concluded in a fit of petulance, "to get a cheque book of his own?" My husband doesn't care to be pre-fixed by the indefinite article. He still uses whichever cheque book comes easily to hand, but sometimes, if he's feeling affable, he cuts the little numbers out of the bottom of the cheque.

I didn't see the letter that my husband wrote to the local postmaster after the stamp machine across the road had once again taken his money and failed to deliver the goods, but it must have been a good specimen of the genre. He sat down and wrote it at 11 pm, as soon as he'd come back from the abortive trip to the stamp machine, and then he went straight down the road and pushed it through the door of the post office. At 9 o'clock the next morning there was a knock at the door and there was a large, beaming GPO official bearing a 3p stamp.

This arrived the other day from a Frenchman, Dr X I'll call him.

"Dear Dr Fenwick, Dr Y (another Frenchman of some distinction) has asked me to present, at our next meeting of the EEG Society, your contribution at the past EEG conference in Marseilles. Would you kindly send me some copies of your communications or, better, some important slides, so that I can present them to our members?"

Well now, one is all for international scientific co-operation, but this did seem too good an opportunity to miss. We thought we might send off something like this, although if anyone could improve on it perhaps they'd let me know.

"Dear Dr X,

Thank you for your letter, and I am looking out my papers for you to give. By a truly astonishing coincidence, the Editor of *World Medicine* has asked me to contribute the paper on artefacts of the EEG in pregnant rabbits, which you presented so impressively at the recent Marseilles conference. I'd be glad if you could let me have your notes – 2,000 words or so should be adequate – and a couple of photographs as he pays extra for those. Thanking you, in anticipation."

I hope it isn't a dying art, chiding letter writing. I'm always pleased when I see the next generation practising it. We discovered our middle child, one day, sitting at the kitchen table writing to the Queen. "Dear Queen," she wrote, "How much pocket money do your children get? I should think about 50p. I hope you have a nice holiday, Love Natasha." Maybe her address was a bit indecipherable, because weeks went by without a reply. She used to belt downstairs every morning and sift through the post, and then come stomping sourly into breakfast muttering, "That Queen..." I was a bit apprehensive when I discovered her laboriously writing away at the kitchen table again a couple of months later. She's a short-tempered child and I was afraid she might descend to truculence and lèse-majesté, but I needn't have worried. The letter she wrote was a perfect example of its kind, combining a hint of mild reproof with an easy let-out. "Dear Queen, I was wondering why you had not replied to my letter. Perhaps you are still on holiday."

And it got results, because she had a foot square envelope from Buckingham Palace by return of post. She writes quite regularly to the Queen now, and always gets a polite reply, but I have noticed that the envelopes are getting smaller and smaller. It will be interesting to see whether Her Majesty has a nice line in chiding letters too.

26

The gentle art of self defence

Rub me up the wrong way these days and I am more than a little likely to send you sprawling in the dust with a mere twist of my right ankle and grind my heel in what our instructor Uncle Tony euphemistically calls your spectacles. If you're lying on your back so I can't get at your kidneys, that is.

Things are tough around Herne Hill. If you took everything you read in the South London Press to heart you'd never dare go down your own garden path. "When they put the rates up last time they said it was because it was a nice area," I heard someone complaining the other day. "So I went round to the Town Hall and said to them, well how come they keep on kicking in the off-licence window?"

Then my friend Patricia next door said we ought to go to this course in Self Defence for Ladies, run by Lambeth Amenity Services as part of their Learn a Sport programme. I told her I had an essentially non-combative nature and suffered from a frozen shoulder and approaching middle age but she said that was the whole point; nobody ever mugged healthy young aggressive-looking Amazons did they?

Patricia said it only cost £1.50 for half a dozen lessons and they provided all the equipment, which I took to mean things like those two-handled springs to encourage muscle development. But it turned out that what they meant was a large rubber mat and a selection of white canvas judo suits with calf-length baggy trousers and wrap-over jackets. Tony said he'd be glad if we all kept our bras, on as the jacket tended to flap a bit until you got the hang of tying your judo belt and we didn't want to get him all excited. Tony himself had a black belt and his assistant Keith an orange one, and a plump little Italian lady struggling to get her white one in a decent knot said a bit nervously that she was a grandmother and she hadn't realised it was judo she'd come here to learn. Tony said reassuringly, well, it wasn't really judo, not strictly, more a mixture of judo, karate, and all-in street fighting.

How many social workers here, he said next, and three out of twelve of us put up their hands. Not as many as usual, he said; the last course it had been half a dozen. Social workers and teachers, that was what he always had most of. They needed it for their work. First thing we had to learn was how to fall. Dead easy here because of the rubber mats, but the principle was just the same on concrete although of course it would hurt a bit more. The main thing was to avoid head injury, so when we fell backwards we must tuck our chins in and fling our arms out at 45° to hit the ground first and absorb the shock.

When we'd all practised this for a bit he showed us how to avoid head injury when we fell forwards, by flinging ourselves over in a kind of sideways forward somersault so that we landed on one of our shoulder blades. After all this none of us could move much without wincing, although none of us had head injuries, so we took a break while Tony went over the legal aspects of self-defence, explaining the difference between common assault (giving someone a bit of a shove), actual bodily harm (pulling a bit of his hair out), and grievous bodily harm (knocking six of his teeth out and kicking his ribs in). Don't worry about the legal angle when it comes to it, Tony told us. It's him or you and you can't afford to be too sensitive. When you've bashed his head in on the pavement, don't hang around looking at the blood and saying Aaargh: cut and run before he gets up again and socks you one.

The worst part of the course was when Tony made us get into pairs and practise holds and throws on each other. Naturally everyone wanted to pair up with the small weak Italian grandmother, but I always ended up with Patricia who is an ex-nurse and doesn't know her own strength. Her forward roll was the best in the class and, what's more, she'd practised a stranglehold on Tony till his eyes started to bulge and he had to flap his arms around to tell her to stop. I didn't much fancy tossing her over my right shoulder and sitting on her head but still less (much, much less, actually) did I like the idea of her doing it to me.

Sometimes Tony would ask the class about their own real-life experiences so that they could re-enact them and see what they ought to have done, because a surprising number of the class had joined the course because they'd suffered some nasty mugging or rape or near-rape, and sometimes he'd act out a scenario with Keith, who was always the one who came off worst. This chap, he'd say, comes up in front of you and makes a grab for your handbag. Fend him off with your left arm, quick jab in the stomach with your right fist, whirl round into the crook of his arm, wristlock on and lean forwards so that over he goes, all backwards on top of him smashing his ribs.

"What if he punches you then?" somebody asked.

Tony looked aggrieved.

"Look," he said, "this chap's in a lot of pain. You've winded him. You've smashed his head in on the pavement. Now you've sat on his chest and crushed six of his ribs. He's not going to punch you."

What if he does, she insisted, so he demonstrated a stranglehold on Keith by locking his forearms round his neck, and a neat Commando trick involving pressure points somewhere in the neck that he said we weren't to practise because it could lead to brain damage.

Of course a lot of this sort of thing, Tony said, was for the open spaces – OK for Clapham Common but in a dark alleyway you'd have no room for manoeuvre. For that you needed the small-arms technique he'd teach us later on – bunches of keys, nail files, thumbs in the eyes. Meanwhile, keep out of alleyways and he'd show us how to kick, aiming with the side of the foot, not the toe, so we weren't so likely to miss. He could teach us to kick them in the teeth like Joanna Lumley but it would take a bit longer, and anyway it's more effective below the belt.

What with the arm-holds and wrist-holds and knowing how to dislocate an opponent's thumbs if he tried to strangle you from behind and dislocate his shoulder from another very complicated position that looked like something out of the Kama Sutra, we all felt pretty aggressive by the end of the course though we agreed it might be a bit different if we ran into trouble without our rubber mats outside Lambeth North tube station on the way home.

"The trouble with my clients," said one of the social workers thoughtfully, "is that they're not going to lay off for a couple of minutes if I say 'wait while I put my judo suit on'."

Tony gave us a final warning against the dangers of over-confidence. When you are attacked, he said, don't just look at them all defiant saying "I've Done Self Defence". They're not going to stand there saying "Cor" and you'll have lost the element of surprise.

27

The importance of being non-obsessional

~~~

I once met a woman who ironed nappies. When I asked her why she did it, she said it was because it made them square. Aesthetically, I can appreciate square nappies as well as anyone, but they're something I'm not prepared to make a good many sacrifices for. On a 0-5 Ironing Rating Scale I would probably score around two, in front of the people who only do the bits of their husband's shirts which show, but way behind the pyjama and tea-towel and vest and nappy ironers.

Not that I don't envy them, some of the time, for I should like to live graciously. Or at any rate more graciously than I do. "I wish I could live like you," said a friend, delicately picking her way through the hall one day, "but Edward wouldn't like it." Kindly disposed friends tend to show towards my housework the attitude traditionally reserved for a woman whistling, or a dog standing on its hind legs; they are surprised to find it done at all: they don't expect it to be done well. They assume that there are Higher Motives, not easily discernible perhaps, but still unimpeachable, behind the dust or debris or the dead flowers. "How clever of you not to sweep up the leaves," said the people who came to dinner last Saturday and had to wade through a colourful autumnal mass of Virginia creeper to reach the front door. "They're so beautiful." They were, too, and I'm always ready for a rationalisation. By the time they'd finished complimenting me I realised that those of us on the fringes of Greater London, with trees, have a duty to keep our October paths unswept for the benefit of less rural friends from Knightsbridge or Kentish Town. Someone else once remarked that that the place reminded him of a farmhouse. I can't think what he meant, in the middle of SE24, unless it was the way the guinea pig trots in and out of the drawing room, nibbling the fringes on the Persian rug.

Of course, not everyone's so tolerant. My mother-in-law still remembers the time I referred to my husband's silver tankard as pewter, and it was no defence to say that it looked like it. Don't run away, though, with the idea that I dislike housework. I quite like it, the way I do it, and I much prefer it to doing somebody else's routine work: letter-writing, say, or filing, or computing. For one thing, you can always do it tomorrow. It's the importance it assumes for other people that irritates. They talk about "Making the Beds", as though it was a piece of construction work comparable to the Sydney Opera House. "You ought to try duvets," they say, "they save so much time. You just pull the bed together and there you are." What's new, what's new?

But I should like to have been born obsessional. I should like to have the order and method in my life that others manage to achieve. I should like to be like the friend who once told us, "We have lunch at 12.30 on Saturdays." To be able to predict with such assurance when lunch will be on any day at all, let alone Saturday, a thoroughly unreliable, unpredictable day, seems to me a marvellous, enviable thing. Doctors consider obsessionalism to be a neurotic trait, I remind myself every now and then, but really I know they're wrong. Probably they are just jealous, like I am. There might be an ingrained, inherited streak in me somewhere, if I could dig it out and cultivate it. Not from my mother – I suspect she's like me, but better at hiding it. She woke up once, clinging to my father. "I've had a terrible dream," she said, "I was in the kitchen, trying to make myself a drink, and I couldn't. There was rice in the tin marked coffee and sugar in the tin marked tea." My father looked bewildered. "But there is," he said.

With a bit of luck I might have an obsessional gene or two from my grandmother. She used to make ginger biscuits and each biscuit was three inches in diameter and weighed half an ounce. It weighed half an ounce because she cut off a piece of dough and trimmed it and weighed it on her scales until that was what it weighed, and there was no cheating by weighing a two-ounce lump and cutting it into four, either. All this sort of thing takes time, of course, which is one reason why I'm not as obsessional as I might be. My grandmother never cut a piece of string in her life, no matter now enticing the contents of the parcel. She undid every knot and wound it into a neat little ball, and put it away in a Terry's Old Gold chocolate box labelled String (Oddments), in the left-hand front corner of the drawer, next to the one marked Candles, which contained candles. Whenever there was a fuse or a power cut at home, it was always quicker to nip round to grandmother's to borrow a candle rather than hunt around in the dark for our own.

If I were obsessional, I'd be like that. I wouldn't just sling the leftover garlic butter into an empty butter-dish and bung it into the fridge. I'd put it into an old yoghurt pot, with a lid on, and I'd label it Garlic Butter and I'd put it in the back right-hand corner of the top shelf in the fridge, where the leftover garlic butter always goes. Then I wouldn't make it into coffee butter icing when I came across it three weeks later.

A non-obsessional has to know her own limitations. She has to realize that she can never marry the sort of man who hangs his own suits up, and that she can't cook Christmas puddings in polythene basins, because when she boils them dry the polythene melts. It isn't only the one-year stands in hospital houses, which have made me the fastest interior decorator in the NHS. We have some friends who re-built their house around themselves from top to bottom: carpentry, plumbing, plasterwork, the lot. All done perfectly. Whenever they were tempted to cut corners, skimp the rubbing down, filling in, finishing off, they called it "Doing a Fenwick". If a thing is worth doing, we non-obsessionals say to ourselves, it's worth doing fantastically quickly, so that we can get on with the next thing, which is equally worth doing.

28

Let's enrich the lingo

~

"Keep up the spirits of your patient with the music of the viol and the psaltery, or by forging letters telling of the death of his enemies, or (if he be a cleric) by informing him that he has been made a bishop, or (if he be an Arab) by discoursing on the virtues and the habits of the camel."

That's an aphorism and it comes from the *Faber Book of Aphorisms*, which someone gave me for Christmas. Six months ago I couldn't have told you what an aphorism was; now I'm never at a loss for a telling opening phrase. Henri de Mondeville said it, or rather he said it all but the last bit about the Arab, which I added myself. But he certainly would have said it if he'd been saying it now instead of whenever it was that he did say it. Who Henri de Mondeville was and what else he said and when he said it I don't know, though I'd very much like to. He doesn't appear in Encyclopaedia Britannica, which has every fact known to man except the one you actually want to look up, and he isn't mentioned in Bartlett's Familiar Quotations. My own feeling is that he was a Trappist monk, goaded into making this one outburst after a session of bloodletting by a particularly lugubrious GP and thereafter relapsing into silence.

There are 5,744 words in Arabic relating to the camel. This is even worse than the Eskimos, who have 120 words for snow. The Arabs also have 80 names for honey, 200 for serpent, 500 for lion (which is surprising really, though I suppose lions may once have ranged more widely over Arabia than they do now), and 1,000 for sword. The book I got these very interesting facts from says these are all subjects on which the Arab mind is strongly and persistently bent. I have a friend who is learning Arabic in preparation for a three-year stint in Saudi Arabia, but I haven't told her all this because, what with not being allowed to drive or show her legs in public and having to smuggle booze into the country in lead-lined coffins, I thought she had enough to worry about. But I did think I ought to bring it, together with Henri de Mondeville's aphorism, to the attention of the staff of the classy private medical emporium in St John's Wood, which has Arabian television piped into all the bedrooms. It's nice to be able to relax your patients with inconsequential chatter.

It all points up the poverty of the English language, though. It used to be much gaudier a few hundred years ago. Dame Juliana Berners, prioress of the nunnery of Sopwell in the fifteenth century and the reputed author of the Book of St Albans, is very firm about the proper use of collective nouns. We are to say: "A congregcyon of people, a hoost of men, a felyshyppynge of women and a bevy of ladyes, a muster of peacockys, a watche of nyghtyngalys, a flyghte of doves, a slewthe of beerys, a gagle of geys, a pontyfycalate of prelates, a dronkenshyp of cobblers and a bomynable syght of monkes". She won't have any sloppy talk about carving game for the table either. Instead "A dere was broken, a chekyn frusshed, a cony unlacyd, a curlewe unjointyd, a heron dysmembryd, a peacocke dysfygured, a samon chynyd, a hadocke sydyd and a breme splayed."

So much food now, like sausages and fish fingers and spaghetti bolognaise, lands on the table already dysmembryd, unjointyd, dysfygured beyond recognition, that it's hardly surprising that these picturesque terms have died out, but it's a pity all the same.

There are ominous signs that we are heading for an economic word crisis. It's the only explanation for the way those available are so often forced into untenable positions. "When I use a word," Humpty Dumpty said in rather a scornful tone, "it means just what I choose it to mean – neither more nor less." Well, yes, a very sensible attitude under the circumstances and, once one accepts it, all sorts of things are clarified, like why they call it the London Park Hotel when all it overlooks is the Metropolitan Tabernacle and the Elephant and Castle, and why Harold Wilson, in answer to the question, "Prime Minister, what would you say have been your chief political faults?" should say, "In the first place I'm very forgiving and in the second I'm outstandingly loyal."

One solution might be to increase word imports from the continent. They have some awfully good words over there. There was a time, just after a rather incident-ridden motoring holiday, when I knew the word for exhaust pipe in six continental languages and every one of them sounded more interesting and evocative and altogether more likely to conjure up the sheer essence of exhaust pipe than exhaust pipe does. The only one I can remember now is auspuff, or something very like it, which is the German version. Not only is it a much more explicit word than exhaust pipe, but there's only one of it, which is presumably why the French imported le picnic instead of going on about le dejeuner sur l'herbe. For this week's word import I'd like to nominate nachtbummel, which my mother brought home from her German evening classes. It's a sort of German way of talking about having a night out on the tiles. Or, as my mother puts it, bumming around at night. Very handy; very succinct. Any German scholars who want to take issue on it, please don't write to me but contact mother's tutor at the Nelson Poly. And a very good nachtbummel to you all.

I was quite wrong about Henri de Mondeville being a Trappist monk. 40 years on we have Wikipedia, which is a huge advance on Encyclopaedia Britannica for almost everything. It told me straight away that Henri de Mondeville (c1260-1320) was a medieval French surgeon who made a significant number of contributions to anatomy and surgery and was the first French man to author a surgical text, "La Chirurgie." And, while we are being precise, its definition of an aphorism: "a concise, terse, laconic, and/or memorable expression of a general truth or principle."

29

Mean Streak

When my built-in obsolescence occurs, and if the Great Manufacturer ever gets around to making a new, improved, jumbo-sized, Mark II version of Me, then I hope He leaves out the mean, Lancashire streak. It is not – I hope it is not – immediately apparent to the naked, uncritical eye, though friends who dine with us regularly may eventually notice how often they are offered moussaka, lasagne and other derivations of mince, and how seldom lobster thermidor or *filet de boeuf en croute*. In fact, I tell myself, as I would most certainly tell anyone else who commented on it, this is a matter of economics rather than tight-fistedness, that I am at the worst thrifty, but really, I am not so sure. Thrift is an uneasy virtue, which, if you take your eyes off it for a minute, degenerates into downright stinginess.

This mean, Lancashire streak of mine (as he likes to call it) seems worse, of course, by comparison with my husband's manic, wilful extravagance (as I like to call it). Whenever either of us is blessed with a new godchild there is a grim, silent race to see whether I can get down the Portobello Road for a second hand napkin ring before he gets round to Cockburn and Campbell to lay down a case of port. There are occasional role reversals though. I may refuse to put on the central heating until ice crystals form on the sitting room carpet but at least I don't work out the cost on a per capita basis, which means we can't have it on during the week when only I'm at home, just at weekends when he is.

It would be easier to cope with, this meanness, if it were consistent or predictable. It has its obvious, domestic side – the stockpot simmering away on the stove, the plastic bags of breadcrumbs from the tail ends of old loaves stuffed into the deep freeze and please don't tell me how much a week those cost to run. Take care of the pence and the pounds will take off by themselves. Nothing gets wasted in our house – even the rabbit gets last night's lettuce with the French dressing washed off. If only such frugality were not allied to an even stronger streak of pure hedonism it might be better rewarded. What use to turn the heating down if, instead of putting on an extra sweater, you are content to warm up on a bottle of claret?

I'm mean with time, too, terribly mean. If it passes with nothing to show for itself I feel aggrieved. Time is money, I say, which is one of life's most misleading platitudes. Shall I save money by walking to the post office or time by driving? Well, it's only five minutes down the road so it shouldn't take a Maynard Keynes to work that one out but you'd be surprised how often I save a couple of minutes by taking the car, and then get a ticket for leaving it on the yellow line. I save time by never using carbons, too – nasty, flimsy things, fiddling around slipping them between the sheets, tapping the whole lot together, slotting them into the typewriter. If you never read this it may be because the editor's turned it down or it may just be that the GPO's lost the only existing copy.

Some people are even meaner than I am and I love thinking about them – it improves my own image of me.

134

There's a doctor I heard of the other day who's always asking his secretary to bring him a sandwich from the hospital canteen but never actually pays her for it, though every now and then he says, gosh, I suppose I must owe you some money. Yes, you do, £2.59 it is now and she'd be glad of it. And then there was a letter I once read in a magazine from a man who was terribly proud of his wife because when she made a steak and kidney pie she made just exactly the right amount of pastry to cover the pie, so not a scrap was leftover. I think that's dreadfully mean. Don't they ever have jam tarts in their family? Because, as everyone knows, nobody ever sets out to make jam tarts; they don't get out the flour and the rolling pin and say I think we'll have jam tarts today. Jam tarts are what you make because there's a bit of pastry left over from the steak and kidney pie, because you're not the sort of penny-pinching person who mixes only just enough to cover it.

It is not the idea of spending money I dislike, only the actuality. It's the handing over of hard cash that hurts so much. With a purse full of money I'm as close as Shylock, refusing the children ice-lollies, pointing out that the thing about toothpaste is that the tube is never actually completely empty so there's no need to get another one today. I am profligate only for the couple of days before I get to the bank, when I can sign cheques, which is painless, and we can get the ice-lollies at the paper shop and put them on the bill, which gives me a pleasant feeling of reckless extravagance, like Onassis. Credit cards, instant riches, were made for people like me. Only last week I actually picked up the bill for four in a French restaurant and paid it. My husband was pleased. We'd discussed it before dinner and I'd convinced him we couldn't afford to pay for anyone but us, so he thought I'd reformed. But I haven't – it was only because they took Barclaycards. I couldn't have done it in francs.

But because of my own limitations, I really admire a big spender when I come across one. You find them in such unlikely places sometimes. I was in this butcher's shop once in Lancashire, where they should all have been canny and close like me, and there was this little old man, his pension book tucked into his breast pocket, and he was buying a joint of beef. A really magnificent joint of beef, much grander than a sirloin, though possibly not quite as exalted as a baron, a joint to make any table groan and he was buying it with as much nonchalance as if it had been a couple of lamb chops. "My goodness," I said, for it was a situation that seemed to me to call for some comment, although the butcher, too, was taking it well in his stride, "you're going to have a good party with that." He looked me up and down, this little old Lancashire man, eyeing my small packet of mince disdainfully. "Aye," he said, complacently. "Now th' kids 'ave left 'ome, th' wife and I can eat 'ow us likes."

30

Confessions of an addict

⁓

I feel a kind of sneaking sympathy when I pass the Drug Addiction Unit down the hill. I, too, am an addict. Socially acceptable, up to a point, but showing all the classic signs; without my fix I am restless, nervous, twitchy and morose. I am a Print Addict. Like the infant with a junkie mother, I was born hooked. I never had a chance – my father can read his way oblivious through any holocaust you care to mention; it's all in the genes. Riveted by the adventures of Old Lob and his Cow at the age of 4+ (and a good deal more riveting they were than Peter and Jane, let alone Dick and Dora), I travelled rapidly downhill. Heaven to me is half an hour in a traffic jam with a good book; hell is an eternity with nothing to read. Notice I say a good book and not a Good Book. Compulsive readers, like compulsive eaters, are omnivorous and indiscriminating in their tastes. I have read widely, but not too well.

The print addict reads rapidly and with a marked lack of attention, developed in self-defence because so much of his input is so atrocious. In fact, the hallmark of the true addict, as opposed to the person who is merely well read, is the frequency with which he is struck by a sense of déjà vu round about page three. It could be page three, or it could be chapter three or even the *dénouement*, when the faint feeling of familiarity finally jells and he realizes he has read the book before. Possibly twice. The addict will read anything; he picks up the sauce bottle to read the label as automatically as my husband picks up the cutlery to look at the silver mark. He clings nervously to the menu in restaurants when the waiter tries to collect it – while it is considered rude to read a novel when being taken out to lunch, it is permissible to browse occasionally through the entrées and the vegetables.

Addiction is a lowering thing. Given a shot of his particular opiate, the addict's sensibilities are quickly blunted. I have read my way through some of the loveliest scenery in Europe. I have wandered round Chartres with a second-rate detective novel beneath my arm. "We can't feed our baby *and* read, Mrs Fenwick," snapped Sister, whisking my book officiously away. *I* could. Never mind the transfer of immunities or the strengthening of emotional ties; so far as I was concerned, the main advantage of breast-feeding was that it left one hand free to turn the pages.

Going into other people's houses for the first time, I look around edgily till I have located the bookshelves, or the untidy heap they keep the magazines in, then sit down beside it. It's not that I expect the conversation to be boring, and, unless I can think of a very good excuse indeed, I wouldn't dream of picking anything up and actually reading it. But, like the man who's given up smoking but keeps a packet in the house just in case, it gives me a feeling of security to know that it's there. If there's no print in the room at all, I go out into the kitchen to help my hostess and find out where she keeps her cookery books.

The print addict works on the assumption that he may at any time find himself with a couple of minutes at traffic lights, between appointments, at bus stops, stirring the soup, and arms himself accordingly. Whether he is setting off for Antarctica or to fetch the children from school, he is never unprepared and nine times out of ten it pays off. "What do you want that for? You'll have to talk to her when you get there." We were going to visit his mother in hospital. Ten minutes later he was walking three miles across the moors for a can of petrol, but I was all right. It was a Good Book that time: Teilhard de Chardin or War and Peace or something. I might never have got around to it otherwise.

Like some people I know with a box of chocolates, the print addict can't stop till the end of the bottom layer. I began on Thomas Hardy during the term when I was meant to be working for University Entrance. The anxiety level was terrific, but I couldn't stop until I'd scoffed the lot. Oh God, please let this be the last one or I'll never get in. Straight through from Tess of d'Urbervilles to The Mayor of Caster-bridge.

I still have certain principles: I don't read other people's hardbacks in the bath, for example. Buddenbrookes fell in three times and the last two chapters formed *papier-mâché* in the airing cupboard. I must borrow another copy sometime and finish it off. And No Lady, (goes the old Victorian edict), Reads Novels Before Lunch. But I know how easily I could be reduced to the level of the meths drinker. Cast me away on a desert island and I would fall on Barbara Cartland or the S-Z volume of the London telephone directory with gratitude and avidity.

The addict is ceaseless in his search for print, however unpromising the terrain. In the ante-room of the chapel of a boys' Borstal (they were doing EEG recordings in the chapel. It seemed to be the only available place), I found, buried deep beneath a pile of prayer books, a copy of Ruby M. Ayres. Younger readers, have you heard of Ruby M. Ayres? Her heroines are called Maisie or Dolly; they are winsome, laughing-eyed, dimpled girls, who are the greatest Chums with the hero, Harry, as straight and upright as an English cricket bat. But Harry meets sloe-eyed, rich, petulant Phoebe, and wants to be more than her greatest Chum. Maisie, though heart-sore for some reason she cannot fathom at the thought of losing her Chum, helps him in his courtship like the plucky little brick she is. But, in the penultimate chapter, Phoebe meets Claude, a cad who doesn't know how to hold his bat, and, when we finally leave them, Harry is pressing a kiss (rather a damp, inexpert kiss, one suspects) on Maisie's dimpled cheek. In a boys' Borstal. Think of it. I replaced it carefully near the top of the prayer book pile and wished I could be in chapel on Sunday.

But we addicts lay ourselves open to some terrible situations. However careful, however provident, there may come a time when we find ourselves without a fix, stranded miles from anywhere without even an out-of-date copy of the Good Food Guide. Homeward bound in the BOAC section of Kennedy Airport, I once found myself without a book. I had finished the suitcase-full I'd taken over and I don't think you should borrow intercontinentally, but I wasn't worried, because every airport has a bookstall: usually quite a large bookstall, if it's quite a large airport. It was some minutes before I realized that I'd been round it twice and found nothing but one of those kiosks selling airport flotsam. The first sensations of panic hit me, palms sweating, faint beading on the brow. I went round once more to make sure, and then shot into the kiosk, breathing rather rapidly. After a couple of circuits of this I noticed, tucked away behind the Butterscotch Life-Savers and the gilded plastic models of the Empire State Building, three small shelves of paperbacks. I searched from end to end and back again, scanning first pages and last pages. There was nothing, absolutely nothing, that anyone capable of getting himself across the Atlantic could possibly have wanted to read. My husband came in. He said: "I've ordered you a blueberry muffin in the restaurant." All the way from Saskatoon to Boston I'd been trying to find a blueberry muffin. I said, "There's nothing here I want to read." He said, "There must be." He knows how low my standards are. We both looked and there wasn't. BOAC, how can you put this sort of stuff between your passengers and eight hours over the Atlantic? You ruined my blueberry muffin.

31

Pride in honest prejudice

~

I 've always liked to think there is not a racially prejudiced
bone in my body. So it was a bit disillusioning to discover
the truth, which is that I'm terribly prejudiced against
Australians. Some of my favourite relatives are Australian
– my husband is half-Australian and my children a quarter
Australian and my mother-in-law totally Australian and
I'm very fond of them all, in different ways, but I'm still
prejudiced against Australians. It's mostly because of a
lodger we had called Arthur.

Arthur made me understand why no other country but
Australia could have produced Germaine Greer. He turned
up on our doorstep one December day surrounded by ski
gear, because a friend of his who was a friend of ours had
told him we sometimes took lodgers. Sometimes we do, I
said cautiously, but really to help with the baby-sitting. All
the others had been dear little nurses who looked after
themselves and were no trouble to have around, indeed
rather pleasant. We gave Arthur the room though, and
he even managed the baby-sitting a few times, sitting with
his feet up in the armchair in the playroom, a stack of

beer cans by his side, bribing them all with chocolate to go to bed.

The first day Arthur was with us he made a momentous discovery: the off-licence across the road sold Fosters beer – Forstus he called it. Fosters is something of a religion with Australians. He bought a dozen cans or so and managed to get them all in the fridge by taking out the bacon and sausages. Then, in a state of happy anticipation, he trundled round the kitchen humming some Australian ditty, waiting for them to zero down. After a while I heard the slamming of the fridge door and then the rattling of cutlery in the kitchen drawer. Soon Arthur appeared, wild-eyed, agitated, an unopened can of Forstus in each hand. "Hevencha gorta beer-can opener?" he cried in disbelief. "Doncha drink beer?" Whenever anyone talks of the Mask of Tragedy I think of Arthur, ice-cold Forstus within each grasp and no beer-can opener.

Arthur's cortex had three zones – for beer, sex and skiing – and he became animated when any one of these was stimulated; but most of life's other possibilities passed him by. He came in once when the children and I were watching a film version of Cinderella or some such well-loved fairy tale on television. "What's it about?" asked Arthur and the children gave him a resume of the plot so far. He watched for a bit and then got up and left the room. "It's a bit far-fetched isn'it?" he said over his shoulder as he went.

He had travelled widely for his father's engineering firm and sometimes he'd tell us about the exotic places he'd visited. "Y'd never believe it," he told us once, talking about Japan, "but they make their houses out of a kind of cardboard. Cardboard! Y'd think they could do better than that." "But Arthur," we said, "isn't that, er, you know, because of all the earthquakes?" "I dunno," said Arthur indifferently. "S'pose it could be."

Although he was perfectly capable of looking after himself and had a lot more time than I had, Arthur had the most irritating habit of wandering around the kitchen when I was doing the ironing, holding an armful of shirts and heaving sighs. Sometimes he'd sit down and tell me about a girlfriend he had back in New South Wales who was a domestic paragon and thought the world of him. "She'd do anything for me," he'd say, casting meaningful glances at the iron. "I'll leave the board up for you when I've finished, Arthur," I'd tell him firmly.

Arthur got through women like Forstus; the one he'd just finished could never believe it was all over when, so far as she was concerned, it had only just started. For a couple of days at the end of each affair he wouldn't answer the phone. "If it's for me and it's Edna," he'd shout, "tell her I'm out." "I'm terribly sorry, but I'm afraid Arthur hasn't come in yet," I'd lie to the tearful voice at the end of the phone. "I know he's there, I know he is," poor Edna would sob. "Last week he was sleeping with me. Now he won't even speak to me."

After these conversations I'd go and find Arthur swilling beer with his feet up. "I think you're completely heartless," I'd tell him. "Can't you let them down a bit more gently?" "She'll get over it," he'd say, taking another swig, "they always do." Towards the end of his stay there was a particularly persistent girl who rang up day after day, "But he must see me; he can't go back without seeing me. Besides," she added, a sudden gleam of hope in her voice, "he'll have to see me. He's got a book of mine."

I was touched by the simple naivety of one who believed that Arthur, of all people, couldn't be such a heel as to go back to Australia with someone else's book, so I agreed that if she came over that evening I wouldn't tell him she was coming, so that he couldn't take avoiding action. When she turned up I shut myself in the kitchen so Arthur had to answer the door. He had her out of the place and back to East Finchley in just over five minutes. I don't know whether she ever got her book but when I came out of the kitchen he was busy unwrapping a huge, gift-wrapped volume of Impressionist painters. "She bought me a farewell present," he said smugly. She can't have known him very well. Arthur wouldn't have known a Cezanne from a naked Japanese wrestler.

What with the women and the skiing and the Forstus, Arthur's holiday trip became so prolonged that some time in February he got a letter from his father demanding his instant return. Arthur was doleful. "They want me back stright awhy," he told us. "Mother's ill and business isn't too good at the moment and Dad says I've got to come back immediately and help him run the firm. I'll heveter leave on Friday." There was a long pause while the tiny cogs in Arthur's mind whirred and clicked. "I think I'll go by boat," he said.

When he went back to Australia he left behind a series of Japanese postcards with enormous, almost naked wrestlers on them; the children found them and one of them took them to school, because they were doing Japan. At the Open Evening the Japanese table was all laid out beautifully with a fan and a kimono and dainty porcelain cups and a flower arrangement, but Arthur's postcards weren't there. They never sent them home either. He also left his ski boots in the attic when he went and promised to return this year. I quite look forward to it in a way. A really good prejudice is so self-indulgently satisfying.

32

One degree under

〜

There are many people who go through life without the aid of a clinical thermometer. I admire them enormously, but I'd love to know how they overcome the problem of self-assessment – how they manage to distinguish the insidious onset of disease from a hangover or a mere disinclination to get out of bed. In our family there are well-established conventions governing the interpretation of the thermometer reading, and everyone knows exactly how ill he's entitled to feel at a given temperature: 100, sympathy, 101 bed, 102 doctor. That's for me – the equivalent readings for him are 98.7, 98.8, 98.9, (I'm joking of course).

It occurs to me, as I fumble around the bathroom cabinet for a thermometer in the middle of the night, that there are two significant moments of freedom in a woman's life. The first when the last child is weaned and she realises that she no longer has to choose her clothes solely because they expand round the middle or unbutton down the front. The second – and this revelation comes like a blinding flash as I see the thermometer register 99.9 – is when the youngest child starts school and she can, for the first time in a decade or so, actually enjoy an occasional spot of mild ill-health.

So I lie there in bed, listening to the rain drumming on the bedroom ceiling through the holes in the roof, and contemplate my good fortune. What an excellent temperature 99.9 is. Any lower and I would hardly be justified in going to bed. Any higher and I might start to feel too ill to appreciate it. With admirable foresight the previous day, having sensed through a general malaise that something of the sort might be going to happen, I have been to Sainsbury's and ironed enough shirts for the rest of the week. It is only Tuesday; I shall miss two committee meetings and, if properly nurtured, be quite better for the weekend's social engagements.

"I think I've got 'flu, I tell my husband in the morning, unselfishly waiting till he's had his strengthening cup of tea before handing him the thermometer with its unanswerable verdict. He glares at it disbelievingly, shakes it till the mercury disappears further into the bulb than the makers ever intended, and thrusts it into my mouth, eyes glued to his watch, hand poised to snatch it back the second the statutory half-minute is up. No use at all – 100.1 – he sits bowed, defeated, a man about to be overcome with domesticity beyond the call of duty. I feel sorry for him. "I don't feel too bad," I say. "I can easily get up and do breakfast." This is true, though I am perhaps not too unwilling to let it appear as martyrdom. The prospect of a guiltless day reading novels, in bed, unfettered by child, makes me feel benign and cheerful.

The eldest child comes in just then, cheeks flushed, clutching her throat. "It's my tonsillitis again," she says. I am outraged to find her temperature is almost as high as mine. "You'll be company for each other," says my husband, looking slightly more cheerful. I give the others their breakfast and join my daughter back in bed, but somehow the joy has gone out of it. Something noisy is happening downstairs and, after a moment, my son comes in and stands by the bed playing with his Lego. When he's fixed the wheels on he says, calmly, "Natasha's been sick."

I deal with this and tuck the second child up beside her sister in my bed and then it is time to send the third one off to wait on the corner for his lift to school. I've hardly shut the door behind him than he's back again, weeping, all bare-legged and pathetic in the pouring rain, but sympathy is not the emotion uppermost in my mind. *"There is absolutely nothing wrong with you at all,"* I say, before the little fellow has a chance to open his mouth. *"You are going to school."* Between sobs, he explains. He's not ill at all. He's only five and this is the first time he's had to go to school without his sisters, and he just doesn't want to wait on the corner, by himself, in the rain. Overwhelmed with relief and remorse I put a plastic mac over my dressing gown, slip on a pair of wellingtons and wait with him till the car comes into sight.

After that I am so pleased to get back to bed that I scarcely care that it has both daughters in it and a pile of trousers with no pockets, which someone has thoughtfully placed on the end of it, in case I feel too ill to read. The younger daughter looks pleased. She is holding out to me some familiar scraps of green and red felt. "You'll be able to make my elephant," she says eagerly. "I'll get your sewing basket." Some evil-minded friend gave it to her for her birthday; it has to be cut out, sewn and stuffed, as if I didn't have enough to do. I try to explain to her that, whereas I feel just able to lie back absorbing print, I am really not up to making felt elephants. Then the front doorbell goes. That's not quite true. The front doorbell doesn't go because it hasn't worked for 18 months. What actually happens is that somebody thumps on the door and then pushes it open and shouts in the hall. All our visitors do this, except the ones who don't know us well enough to know that the bell never works, and they sometimes go away and ring us up from the phone box across the road, to see if we're in.

The person shouting in the hall is Mr Davies, our friendly neighbourhood artisan. He has come to do the last bit of wallpapering round the well of the stairs, which I can't quite reach. Most of the time he spends putting a new roof on our house, but we have this long-standing arrangement with him that one day when it is too wet to do the roof he will do the wallpapering instead. There have probably been other rainy days in the last three months, but this is the one he has chosen. Some of you may be thinking that three months is a long time to be putting a new roof on a house but there are good reasons for this. The first is that by mischance the tiles were delivered to the wrong address and had to be moved piecemeal 200 yards down the road. The second is that by further mischance, the area of roof to be covered turned out to be greater than the area of tiles ordered. The third mischance was that half-way through the job Mr. Davies lost his head for heights and he had to hand over the work to an unreliable team of itinerant Irishmen from Croydon. It's awful the way some people's lives are dogged by misfortune.

Mr Davies, a kind man, urges me back to bed and goes off to mix his paste. A few minutes later he's back. He can't find a bucket to mix it in although I described to him its exact location behind the waste-bin. In the end I get out of bed to show him and it isn't there. Of course it isn't there. It isn't there because it is up in the attic sitting under one of the places where Mr Davies ran out of tiles, along with every other saucepan and casserole dish in the house. For three months we've been able to have people for dinner only on fine evenings. We solve the problem by replacing the bucket with the only receptacle left in the house: our lodger's saucepan. I hope it will have stopped raining by the time she's hungry.

Back to bed again, I lie back exhausted on the pillows and take my temperature again: 100.9 and no wonder. "Why aren't you doing my elephant?" says the younger daughter. "You're always saying you haven't got time to do my elephant and here you are lying here doing nothing at all. You could easily do my elephant."

A few minutes later Mr Davies comes in and says what about a nice cup of tea, or should he make it – only he's all pastey?

After that the girls decide they could eat a few fish fingers. I can tell they're feeling better because they are practising headstands and back-bends all over the bed. After lunch I try to take my temperature again but one of them has stood on the thermometer.

My husband goes over to the chemist when he arrives home and buys a new thermometer, all marked in centigrade. "You're getting along splendidly," he tells me. "You'll be able to get up tomorrow. It's 37.9."

We haven't worked out a code of practice for that yet.

33

Lessons for life

~

Children are more obsessional than trade unionists about maintaining parity and differentials. "She had a cat when she was 8 and now I'm 8 and you say I can't have a cat because we've got two already. It's not *fair*." That must be why psychologists say having pets is good for children. It teaches them about life. The unfairness of it, I mean, not just birth and death and that sort of thing. So far as birth and death go, there's a certain amount of overkill in the lessons they learn; it's all so very unlike the home life of a well-ordered household within the welfare state.

There was the awful, awful Christmas, as we drove down from the North in torrential rain, when we stopped to mend a windscreen wiper and I inadvertently slammed the car door on small, black and white cat Figaro. We drove off the motorway and found an oak wood to bury him in and the cat's owner was very, very nice to me and kept sobbing, "Don't cry, Mummy, I know you didn't mean to murder him." Then when we got home there was a note from Patricia, our next door neighbour, pinned to the door, which said, "Please come and see me without the children." She'd been in *loco parentis* to the guinea pig and I guessed what had happened before she'd even told me. Willie, the last of a long line of short-lived guinea-pigs, the only one to die of senility, though he had gastroenteritis, too, had passed away on Christmas Eve in front of their Aga – peacefully, so far as one can ever tell with a guinea-pig. He had survived for so long because he had a wily nature and a fair turn of speed, or perhaps just because the largest cat had tired of an unvarying diet of guinea pig.

They are my favourites, the guinea pigs: appealing creatures, so perfectly symmetrical about their horizontal axis that until they move it's impossible to tell which way they're facing. And because they lead a pleasant, indoor life, able to escape and range the house with their little clockwork trot, they make me feel less guilty than the rabbits. The rabbits lead a dingy, solitary, unpetted existence in their hutch: not so bad when there were two of them, but Sapphire left home some months ago and now Ruby's on her own. We put a notice in the sweetshop window asking if anyone had seen a large white rabbit called Sapphire, though he didn't answer to it. Someone had – they'd found what was left of him in a gutter on the other side of the main road, but I didn't tell the children. It was nicer to think of brave, adventurous Sapphire setting off to seek his fortune in the park and they played along with this, though I think they guessed the truth. He was always a great escaper, Sapphire. When we put them in their run in the garden he used to tunnel out as though it were Colditz, while Ruby just scrabbled delicately at the wire until she'd clawed her way through. It wasn't until the eldest child read *Watership Down* and told us that only female rabbits burrow, that we realised we'd been making a lot of false assumptions about those rabbits. It just shows how careful you have to be about believing sexual stereotypes. It explained the difficulty we'd had getting Ruby pregnant with Benjamin next-door though. Benjamin's not a very *masculine* sort of rabbit, I used to think, watching huge white Ruby chasing the poor little fellow round the run and trying to mount him. Actually, I thought there was something wrong with both their hormones, but of course it was more fundamental than that.

Usually when the rabbits escape they go straight through the holes in the fences to either of the gardens next door, which proves that rabbits have more intelligence than one would normally credit them with, as these gardens have a greater variety and profusion of attractive plants than they can find in their own. I would like to pay tribute, now, to the tolerance these neighbours display under repeated provocation by marauding rabbits, but I do try to get the rabbits out before they discover they're there, if I possibly can, because I know they can't keep on displaying it for ever. In the middle of one of the front lawns is a large, circular flowerbed and very early one morning we discovered Ruby sitting in the middle of this, chewing lupins. I deployed those forces who were up and dressed around the circumference of the flowerbed and tried to dislodge Ruby with the end of an umbrella, which was the only implement long enough to reach her that I could find on the spur of the moment. At each prod Ruby merely hopped six inches out of reach and went on grazing till I'd rushed round the other side of the bed. After a while, a passing citizen on his way to some early morning shift paused to watch the activity and, assessing our difficulties in a trice, jumped over the wall and waded straight into the middle of the flowerbed, heedless of the primulas beneath his boots. He picked up Ruby, who was taken unawares by this sudden reversal of policy, and handed her to me politely, saying, "Rabbits is frightened of umbrellas."

It's the middle child who has the rabbits and the guinea pigs, the eldest who has the cats. The youngest is fobbed off with goldfish – the dullest pets imaginable, of course, but they have the advantage that so long as you discover Alonzo floating on his side looking even more glassy-eyed than usual before the child does, you can rush down to the pet shop and buy another Alonzo before the child comes home from school. In this way, Alonzo develops a totally unfounded reputation for longevity, with time the child grows fonder of him than his personality warrants and the end, when it does come, is a shock to everyone, for Alonzo by this time is considered immortal. In our case it happened that one of the cats, feeling sportif rather than ravenous, fished the creature out of its bowl and abandoned it on its owner's bedroom floor, to be squashed beneath his bare feet as he leapt out of bed next morning. How much less traumatic to have come to terms with death within the confines of a goldfish bowl.

34

The Cat Lady

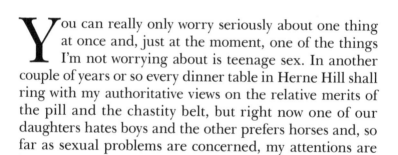

You can really only worry seriously about one thing at once and, just at the moment, one of the things I'm not worrying about is teenage sex. In another couple of years or so every dinner table in Herne Hill shall ring with my authoritative views on the relative merits of the pill and the chastity belt, but right now one of our daughters hates boys and the other prefers horses and, so far as sexual problems are concerned, my attentions are bound up with the cat.

Not the great big tabby cat who came with the house; he has had no lustful thoughts for years and cannot understand what the fuss is about. It's the little, cream-coloured Siamese cat who, at irregular, unpredictable and ever diminishing intervals, possibly connected with sunspots or the phases of the moon or high tides on the river Thames, is transformed from a demure, face-washing, fireside-sitting pussy into one huge erogenous zone with a sexual drive that makes Casanova look like Little Jack Horner. Her turbulent passions are accompanied by a continuous harsh wail of agony, matched in intensity only by the cry of a newborn infant demanding food and which, the first time it happened, sent my husband hotfoot and red-eyed to the vet. I had taken the children to their grandmother's and the ferment of the cat's desires had kept them both awake all night.

"My cat," he said, laying the squirming, howling creature on the vet's table, "is mortally ill."

The vet gave a loud, unfeeling laugh.

"Your cat," he said, "is on heat." My husband blanched.

"Is it always like this?" he asked.

"Always," said the vet. "Siameses are noted for it."

"Does it last long?" said my husband.

"With Siameses," said the vet, thoughtfully, "it's usually about a week."

"Does it happen often?" said my husband.

"With Siameses," said the vet, "about every three weeks. Sometimes oftener," he added.

Which is why, some weeks later, we found the cat lady.

The cat lady had been recommended to us as a breeder of Siamese cats of some distinction; she had not only a champion available for stud purposes but also a grand champion. Ever modest and not wishing to over-reach ourselves in our first breeding venture, we settled for the champion. Reginald Clippertree he was called. What was our cat called, asked the cat lady. We looked at each other, nobody wishing to reply. "Cuddly," said our elder daughter eventually. After all, it's her cat: she christened it.

The cat lady's walls were covered with rosettes, diplomas and certificates of merit. There were Siamese cats all over the furniture and pictures of Siamese cats on all the shelves – Siamese cats with appealing little boys, Siamese cats with endearing little girls and Siamese cats with kittens. There was a lamp base in the form of a plaster Siamese cat and a Siamese cat with a litter of kittens in a washing-up bowl under the table. The cat lady thought the children should see what Cuddly would look like when she was pregnant, so she disappeared upstairs and returned with a cat that looked nine months pregnant. She also brought down a cat with kittens that had been born the previous Sunday, a cat who had delivered that morning and a cat that she said was in labour.

"I expect," said the cat lady finally, "that you'd like to meet Reggie." She left the room again and we all huddled together on the sofa, presenting a united front against the ranks of Siameses pacing the floor, fixing us with glacial stares, waiting for someone to turn their back so they could leap on it. In such a situation even a cat lover might turn phobic: a felinophobe stark, raving mad. We murmured soothingly into the cat basket where Cuddly was being whipped into a frenzy by the overpowering smell of tomcat.

Eventually the cat lady returned, bearing in her arms an animal about five times the size of Cuddly and at least fifty times as malevolent. It was impossible to believe they were the same species, let alone the same breed. Reginald Clippertree's eyes rolled, his tail lashed, every hair stood vertically on the back of his neck. Cuddly's cries grew to a crescendo and my daughter clutched the cat basket protectively to her. "He gets angry," explained the cat lady unnecessarily, "if he can't get at the queen. I would let you stroke him," she went on, although none of us had lifted a finger, "only he'd take your hand off."

We stood around respectfully, trying to look as if we were fighting down an overwhelming urge to stroke Reginald Clippertree. The cat lady gripped him firmly by his back legs and demonstrated all his championship qualities. He was not, to our eyes, a pretty pussy but he had evidently captivated every judge on the Siamese circuit.

"Do you think," said my husband, timidly – and he is not a timid man – "that our Cuddly might, er, win any championships? If we showed her?"

The cat lady gave a merry laugh. "Oh dear me no," she said. "Her eyes are too round for one thing and her nose is too pointed. "Mind you," she added more kindly – like a headmaster saying that, never mind, your child's quite good at woodwork – "her coat's a good colour: a very good, light colour. I've been wanting to breed for that." We got the unmistakable impression that had Cuddly's fur not been up to scratch, the match would have been called off.

We all felt a bit worried when we drove off and left Cuddly to her nuptial doom. "All she wanted was just any old tomcat," said my daughter, tearfully and truthfully, "I don't see why you had to bother getting her a champion."

That evening we rang up for a progress report. "She's very spoilt, isn't she?" said the cat lady severely. "She's really not settling down at all well. She bit me – well, I don't mind that, of course, but she bit Reggie too."

"Oh, I am sorry," I said. "Do you think she's too young, it's too soon; I'd better fetch her home?"

"Oh, she'll come round in the end – virgin queens are often like that," said the cat lady. No wonder Essex never got to first base. "Don't you worry about it at all. Reggie's never failed yet."

When we went to fetch Cuddly back the following weekend the cat lady told us it had all gone splendidly in the end. "It's all done her a lot of good, getting away from home for a bit," she told us firmly. "She was obviously far too tied to mother's apron strings." It's true, it's true; I always have her in by eleven, and we may have stopped the children from coming into our bed but not the cat. When she gets home again I'll give her a latch-key and stop worrying about the big white tom over the fence. It's not just sex I worry about but he once ate one of our rabbits.

I sat down, feeling like a procuress, and wrote the cat lady a cheque for services rendered, and our son, who likes to get his money's worth, eyed her suspiciously and said, "How do you know that he's actually, you know, gone and mated her?"

"Well," said the cat lady, "Reggie's a bit of a show-off. He likes to perform for me when I take him his dinner."

"How many times did he do it?" demanded my son. "How

long did it take him?"

"Hush," I muttered, "Two or three times, I should think. Just to make sure."

"I'm not asking you," said my son, "you weren't there. I'm asking her. I mean just roughly how long? About a minute or two hours?"

The cat lady gave us a mating certificate and a kind of Dr Spock for kitten rearers, which she thought we might need, and all the way home we passed Cuddly from lap to lap because she smelt so powerfully of Reginald Clippertree that no one could stand her for long. For the next two weeks we watched her eagerly for signs of early morning sickness or thickening waistline and she seemed perfectly normal and perfectly happy and perfectly untraumatised by her sexual experience. Then she woke us up last Sunday morning, howling like a banshee and rolling about the floor in sexual frustration. "I thought Reggie Clippertree never failed," said our daughter reproachfully.

We're going to take her back for another try because, after all, it was a very substantial dowry and then she'll just have to take her chance with the white tom over the fence. Meanwhile, please don't expect too much sympathy from me when you go on about how hard it is to stop your daughters getting pregnant. I've got troubles of my own.

35

The new Psychiatry: a feline approach

~

The best place to advertise a litter of kittens is the Exchange & Mart. This is just a gratuitous piece of information I'm tossing your way. You can file it away somewhere if you don't need it at the moment but you may be very grateful to me some day for mentioning it. Nobody told us about it for a long time and we spent a lot of money advertising in all sorts of useless places, and meanwhile the kittens were hanging fire, eating their heads off and driving their mother and me up the wall.

Then one evening the telephone rang – it was the day our advertisement appeared in the South London Press – and the voice at the other end said she'd seen our advertisement about the kittens, so I felt quite excited. She said she was interested because she'd got a Siamese herself. That was nice, I said. A seal point, she said. Oh, ours was blue, I said. Hers was pregnant, she said. She'd had her mated properly, of course. Yogi Bear over at Catford. Did I know him? He'd got ever such a nice nature. I said of course I'd heard of Yogi Bear over at Catford, though I'd never actually met him, but in fact we'd used Reginald Clippertree over at

Maidenhead. Then she said wasn't that rather a long way to go, because she could see from our telephone number we were a lot nearer Catford than Maidenhead. And I said, well yes, but it had seemed like a good idea at the time because we were driving down to Dorset that weekend and thought we could just drop her in on the way down and pick her up on the way back, but we hadn't realised we'd have to leave her there for a whole week, and then we'd had to take her back for a second try so it had been a bit inconvenient really. She said Reginald Clippertree was a good stud though, and I said I'd heard Yogi was good too and then there was a bit of a pause.

After a while she told me her name was Phoebe, so I told her mine was Elizabeth, and then she told me the reason she liked cats was that she was agoraphobic and hadn't been out for four years and cats were very good company when you didn't get out. She said she lived on the Peabody Estate down at Camberwell Green and I felt like saying that I was surprised she'd got agoraphobia if she lived on the Peabody Estate – if I lived on the Peabody Estate I wouldn't be able get out fast enough. It looks like a vast maroon Victorian workhouse and commands a fine view of the meths drinkers on the Green. I said it must be dreadful to be agoraphobic and didn't she manage to get out at all, and Phoebe said well, sometimes she went with her friend who took her to Bingo and, of course, she had to go up the clinic once a week. So I said well, it was a good thing she was having treatment and was it helping? Phoebe said she didn't think it was. She said she didn't think the psychiatrist really understood her. He said it was all in the relationship with her husband. He said her husband had to come along to the clinic with her. He said the trouble was they didn't communicate. He said if her husband came with her to the clinic it might help them to communicate. Phoebe said what the psychiatrist didn't seem to understand was that she didn't want to communicate.

Then I thought of a paper I'd read in some journal where someone had cured somebody of a phobia about high-level lavatory cisterns by making them run round and round the block till they were absolutely exhausted, and in this state they became less phobic about pulling the lavatory chain. I told Phoebe about this and said why didn't she try running up and down the stairs of the Peabody Estate very fast, several times, and then see if she felt more like going out, because, to be quite honest, I was rather taken with the idea of getting one up on Phoebe's psychiatrist and curing her while he was still messing about trying to get her to communicate.

But Phoebe said one of the things about not going out for four years was that she'd put on 4 stone and she didn't think her heart would stand it. She said she'd tried one of the groups though, like Alcoholics Anonymous, where agoraphobics all tried to help each other. It had been started by a very nice agoraphobic called Valerie, but then a very bossy agoraphobic called Dawn had booted Valerie out and taken it over, which wasn't fair when Valerie had started it, and they'd all quarrelled so much among themselves that Phoebe didn't think it was doing her much good, so she'd stopped going.

But she said it had really cheered her up, talking to me, and did I mind if she kept my number and gave me another ring sometime and I said no, not at all, any time she felt like it. And then Phoebe said oh, by the way, the reason she'd rung was to tell me if I wanted to find nice homes for my kittens I ought to advertise them in Exchange & Mart. Not the South London Press. Not a very nice class of person reads the South London Press, Phoebe said.

When I put the phone down, everyone jumped up and down excitedly and said had I sold the kittens to that lady and I said, no, not exactly, but at least I knew how to set about it now.

Phoebe was right about Exchange & Mart – we sold the kittens with no trouble at all. She rings me up about once a week now and we have a nice chat. Not long ago her psychiatrist advised a break in treatment for a few weeks, and Phoebe says it's made her feel ever so much better. She's even taking driving lessons and managed to go over Waterloo Bridge last week, although she used to be terribly phobic about water. She says she wants to get on as much as possible before she has to go back to the clinic. She's afraid the treatment may set her back again.

NORTH OF THE BORDER

36

Water, water everywhere

~

*T*his was written in the summer of 1976, when months of dry weather brought about a drought so severe that crowds cheered at Lord's when a few drops of rain stopped play for a quarter of an hour in mid June. Two months later, with no end to the crisis in sight the Prime Minister, James Callaghan, appointed a drought minister – Denis Howell – whose homespun wisdom raised a few laughs if nothing else. As minister in charge of drought co-ordination, Mr Howell summoned reporters to his home to reveal his own revolutionary water-saving device: a lavatory cistern containing a brick to save water. He also revealed that he was about to save more water by jumping into the bath with his wife. We were on our usual summer holiday in Scotland, where our usual water supply – a tank on the hillside above the house, had dried up completely.

Staggering into the bathroom with yet another 8-gallon can of water from the loch to fill the lavatory cistern, I understand why they call this the Age of Aquarius. Our hearts are only very slightly rent by stories of southerners putting bricks in their lavatories or saving their bath water for their tomatoes. Soft livers, we think. Anyone whose water still comes out of taps is, by my definition, not short of water. Being short of water means bathing in the pool beneath the waterfall, even if, like me, you have never before set foot in Scottish waters. So much more romantic than porcelain and chrome, and even the laundry becomes a pleasurable, peasant-like experience: washing in a bucket of soapsuds beneath the beech trees; rinsing in the constant cold running water of the stream. The stains on the front of my husband's jersey, which have survived two London machine-washes intact, dissolve away, and with them another twentieth century myth.

Lack of water has seldom been our problem on Scottish holidays. If it has occurred, it has more usually been because of a particularly large frog wedged in the outlet pipe of the tank on the moor, which supplies the house. Small frogs, materialising in the sink as if by magic, are commonplace. They do no damage, except to the appetites of visitors. There is an attitude of mind, sustained self-protectively by us all, that our water, filtered through the peat and the heather and with a distinctive taste and colour far more striking than Evian or Malvern waters, is not only harmless and unpolluted, but positively beneficial. Tenants of a nearby holiday cottage, whose landlady had thoughtlessly neglected to give them the necessary brainwashing, were stricken with horror the first time it appeared, brown and murky, from the taps. When they complained, she gave them muslin filters, which kept out most of the livestock, but not the particles of peat. They couldn't take it and demanded their money back and headed south. "Londoners," she hissed after them, righteously indignant. "Getting your water out of sewers."

My mother-in-law's house, an old shooting-lodge, has five bathrooms and seven lavatories, perhaps an indication of the average highland rainfall as much as of a vanished way of life. The farmhouse down the road draws its water from the same moorland tank, but their outlet pipe is at a higher level, so that if there is a water shortage it affects the farm first, rather than the lodge, illustrating the feudal mentality of the Victorians who put the plumbing in. But the occupants of the lodge have seldom had to share their bath water so the tenants can drink, although this year equality has been imposed, because there is no water for anyone. The five bathrooms, the seven loos, stand empty, as magnificent as ever but quite unusable.

It is only years of conditioning that make one expect water to appear automatically at the turning of a tap. Our water lack is merely a technicality, imposing few real problems, because the house, in fact, is almost entirely surrounded by water. Southwards, it faces onto Loch Ruthven, separated from it by the road, three fields, and an acre or so of what is usually bog. Moreover, there is a steep climb down, and subsequently up, and all of this makes us reject it out of hand as a source of water. Round to the west, the bank levels out and the road draws near enough to the loch to make filling easier, though the cows paddling muddily at its edges make the water seem too unpalatable to drink. So usually we avoid this, too, and drive round to the other loch, which lies to the east and belongs to the water board. It forms part of the Inverness supply and is therefore regarded as fit for human consumption.

There are no cows here, but there are always campers, fishing and bathing in defiance of the water board's notice prohibiting camping, fishing, and bathing. We tut-tut to ourselves, because when nothing normally passes along the road but sheep, walking stiff-legged with small, deliberate steps, like stout dowagers whose corns are hurting, two Germans and a small tent seem like an invasion. Down the western end of Loch Ruthven there are never any campers, although it is a most delightful spot. This is because George Ferguson who owns it has developed an infallible method for persuading anyone who does decide to settle there to abandon it in favour of the site he has set up half a mile away behind his house. Here, most profitably for George, they can use real lavatories and plug in their electric shavers and buy their bacon from the camp shop. George inherited the estate from his father, after half a lifetime in the grocery business, and would like to set the whole place up as a commercial venture to rival Aviemore, building holiday chalets and hiring out pedal cycles. He lectures the other joint owners of the loch, a retired colonel, two elderly widows, and a very dour farmer, about the importance of utilising their assets and realising their potential, and raises every Calvinist hair on their heads by attempting such innovations as motorboats on the loch and Sunday fishing.

George's fail-safe system for diverting campers from loch-side to campsite is to send down his gamekeeper, Willie Mackenzie, a benevolent-looking, jovial fellow, who appears beside the offending tent or caravan wreathed in smiles. The campers, startled from the frying of their sausages with the guilty, flustered look of all but the most hardened squatters on someone else's territory, embark on a defensive apologia, but soon relax under the influence of Willie's geniality. Before long they are offering him burnt sausages and Nescafe and asking if the water's fit to drink. They shake hands all round as he rises to go, and he says he hopes they'll pass a very comfortable night. He's hardly gone a yard when he's struck by sudden recollection and turns back to them. "I forgot to mention," he says, smiling as benignly as ever. "If the adders get too troublesome there's a wee field yonder behind the house you can use." Then off he goes, in the sure knowledge that they are all falling over themselves behind him tearing up the guy-ropes.

37

Counting sheep

~

It is apparent to me (one of the advantages of operating from a position of absolute ignorance is that solutions to even the most extremely complex problems are apt to become apparent to you) that as nobody knows exactly how to stop inflation then the only thing to do is to find some way of making it more tolerable to live with. It shouldn't be difficult – there are conditions in which spending large sums of money can be painless, or even pleasant. Playing Monopoly, for instance, or on holiday in other people's countries; in fact, anywhere where one can regard the currency more as tokens than as real cash, not to be taken altogether seriously.

So obviously what is needed is some way to jolly up our attitude towards sterling, to give it an air of sparkle and fantasy that is terribly lacking at the moment. With hindsight it's easy to see that the government made a huge error in going decimal when it did. If it had held off till the beginning of the inflationary spiral, people might not have minded or even noticed the amazing prices they were paying, as their attention would have been so taken up with the arithmetic and the funny coins. At the school jumble sale, immediately after the introduction of our new decimal currency, the public (and the jumble sale public is the meanest in the world) were happily paying 2p and 3p and 4p for old pyjamas, which they could have got for 2d and 3d and 4d the year before.

It's possible, though I don't think it's likely, that the government would be prepared to introduce yet another currency system to take our minds off inflation. Alternatively, they might like to reduce coins of all denomination to the size of the 5p piece, which everyone finds such an infernal nuisance that they are happy to spend it at any price. But there are disadvantages to this, one of which would be that I would have to mend the holes in my husband's pockets. After quite a lot of thought, for which I am charging the government nothing, I have concluded that by far the most attractive solution would be to change, not the coinage but the numbers themselves. What I am advocating, in fact, is a return to the ancient Celtic sheep-counting numerals, which have so much more charm than the rotten lot we've been lumbered with for so long that it would be a positive pleasure to use them, even in an inflationary situation.

Yain, tain, eddero, peddero, pitts, tayter, later, overro, coverro, dix, yain-dix, tain-dix, eddero-dix, peddero-dix and bumfitt. I don't know any more – perhaps there aren't any more, perhaps Celtic shepherds never had more than fifteen sheep, but that's enough to show you what I mean. And while decimal coinage may have met with some chauvinist resentment, I think yain, tain, eddero, peddero, etc, will strike some deep Celtic cord within us all. I'm not offering it as a permanent solution to our economic problems, of course, but I think, for a temporary lifting of the spirits, it might be hard to beat and I would be surprised if anyone wanted to go back to the old lot after a few months' trial. Who, having savoured bumfitt, could ever feel the same about fifteen again?

The discovery that the Celts used a special system of numerals for counting sheep explains something that has always puzzled me, which is why counting sheep is supposed to send you to sleep. Sheep have never seemed to me to be especially soporific – rather the reverse in fact. This is partly because I have spent so many sleepless nights chasing them out of my mother-in-law's Scottish garden.

It wouldn't seem such an unprofitable way of spending the middle of the night if my mother-in-law's garden was of the cultivated or cottage variety, with roses or lupins or canterbury bells. But it is only an extension of the moor itself, although the heather is more luxuriant because the sheep are not allowed to make forays into it, and there is a small plantation of scots pines, by courtesy of a grant from the forestry commission, which have to be sprayed individually each summer to rid them of the fearsome caterpillars of the pine-sawfly, which go through them like locusts, stripping the branches bare. The caterpillars are a real threat, but not the sheep. So, when my mother-in-law tries to rouse us to action in the night, we mutter, irritably, "Oh God, can't it wait till morning?" But it can't, because she evidently feels that unless an instant purge is carried out the sheep will, by morning, have established themselves in impregnable positions, will have become so deeply entrenched that neither negotiation nor brute force will shift them. There are nights when we lie there rigid, listening to the sheep, who are cunning enough to march silently along the heather verge rather than tramp up the drive, but so stupid that they are unable to resist giving each other an occasional soft triumphant baa. Then when my mother-in-law opens our door we dive cravenly beneath the bedclothes, pretending we are asleep, pretending we haven't heard them, pretending they aren't there.

"I'm afraid someone's left the gate open again," says my mother-in-law, sounding more reproachful than apologetic, and we are banished into the night.

I think, probably, that sheep-counting as a cure for sleeplessness was discovered by a Celtic shepherd called Goidel, whose wife, Brython, was (like my mother-in-law) unable to tolerate sheep around her hut or barrow or whatever, during the hours of darkness. Night after night she would shake Goidel awake, hissing "The sheep are in again" into his unresponsive ear, until finally the poor fellow would stagger reluctantly outside to round up his flock, counting them by the gate, for Brython (like my mother-in-law) was sensitive even unto the smallest woolly lamb in the farthest corner of the plot.

"Yain," he would say sleepily, tain, eddero, peddero," and gradually the rhythm and resonance of the sequence would overcome him, "tayter, later, overro, coverro," and, long before the fifteenth or bumfitt sheep had scampered through, he would fall to his knees, lulled into sleep. "I don't like any number under eight," my son said to me firmly, once, and I didn't know what he meant then, but I do now. I don't like them myself, when I come to think of it. They're a dreary, staccato, arrhythmic, illogical lot – even children, who pick up most things pretty easily, have to have a set of perfectly ridiculous rhymes to get them to learn to count. "One, two, buckle my shoe, three, four, knock at the door." I bet Celtic babies lay in their cradles chanting "yain, tain, eddero, peddero" and clutching their toes, and were out counting the sheep before they could walk. It's a very great pity the method was ever abandoned and there's a strong case for resurrecting it, for medicinal if not general usage. Think of the saving to the Health Service in Mogadon and Soneryl if, instead of prescribing hypnotics, doctors just gave their insomniac patients a list of Celtic sheep-counting numerals, with simple instructions. They'd all be asleep in no time at all. Before you could say bumfitt.

After a good many years of this we found a miraculous solution to the problem of invasive sheep. We installed a cattle grid.

38

The monster watcher

Frank Searle stands sternly by the shores of Loch Ness, looking like a younger, stockier David Niven, his telescope poised, ready to investigate any unusual movement in the water, his camera slung around his neck also at the ready, for the monster, if it appears, isn't going to hang around for the likes of you and me to fish our cameras out of the boot of the car and fiddle around with our light meters. This is one reason why Frank Searle has a virtual monopoly on monster photography; this, and the fact that for the last five years, winter and summer, he has lived in a tent on the shores of the loch, maintaining a dawn-to-dusk watch for its rarest form of wildlife.

We have come down here to see him, from our eyrie up on the moors, to get away from the weather. There are days up there when the sky is as blue as the Mediterranean and the loch mirrors the hills on every side. It's a beautiful view when you can see it, but more often there is driving rain, or one wakes to a damp blanket of mist up to the windows and the eerie bleatings of invisible sheep. Usually the wind blows so ferociously round the house that the loch is whipped to a ferment and no child under the age of five can stand upright outside the front door. But whatever it's like it's weather that we have up here: real weather, proper weather, and none of that indeterminate, temperate, insipid stuff that passes for it down in the south. The natives, with misplaced pride, boast that their latitude is more or less the same as Stockholm and only a little further south than Leningrad, that geographically they are part of the North Polar region, that even now, in mid-August, there are pockets of snow in the Cairngorms somewhere to the south and west of us, and that there is no landfall between Thurso and the North Pole.

After a day or so's holiday, the children tire of pitting themselves against the elements, a contest in which they are quite outclassed. Then they bound in, in the morning, ignoring nature's offerings outside the window, urban to the core. Can we go to the park, they say, little faces glowing with excitement at the thought of the swings, the slide, the roundabout, in the tatty little playground on the fringe of Inverness. Look at the hills, the loch, the heather, we say, but hopelessly, knowing ours to be a lost cause against their infant philistinism, that what they really want is the ice-rink, the clock-golf course, the trampolines, the fair, all well laced with ice cream and salt and vinegar crisps. So we decide to concentrate on what is, after the weather and the scenery, the third regional speciality: monsters.

There is a new one this year, at the Nigg yard in the Cromarty Firth, where the whole operation to build the world's largest oil rig reads like a section from the Guinness Book of Records. 'Highland I' weighs 37,000 tons, was constructed in the world's biggest hole, and will be towed to the Forties Field by the world's two most powerful tugs. Certainly she dominates the Firth, although the children complain that from our vantage point on a hill facing the yard they cannot see down the hole, but her size is meaningless until we notice the cars and men and buildings beside her, all dwarfed to insignificance by the vast black web of steel. At 420 feet high, she compares favourably to the Great Pyramid of Cheops (480 feet) or St Paul's Cathedral (489) or even the Washington Monument (555), but could hardly hold a candle to the Eiffel Tower (985), the Empire State Building (1,250) or any television mast you care to mention. Even so, we gaze respectfully, only slightly disappointed that we are too late to see the Queen arriving in Britannia to inspect her, and that the actual launching which we had hoped to see has been postponed a couple of days: because of the weather. We tell the children all these interesting facts about 'Highland I' but, perhaps because they have never seen the Great Pyramid of Cheops or the Washington Monument, they are unimpressed; anyway, they have discovered an adventure playground – the gun emplacements, which guarded the entrance to the Firth during World War II. Enchanted, they spend the next hour exploring the maze of dank subterranean concrete tunnels and flinging themselves down iron ladders coated with thirty years of rust.

The weather does not deter Mr Searle. He merely puts on his oilskins and rolls down the flaps of his tents, one his living quarters, one housing his demonstration of photographs and press cuttings – he has an exclusive and profitable contract with a Glasgow newspaper. These are usually wide open to the public gaze for, like a magician demonstrating that, look he has nothing absolutely nothing up his sleeve, he keeps everything frankly, openly on show. No facilities for secret developing and doctoring of negatives; no papier-mâché models of monsters stuffed away under the brushwood. For there are those who have suggested that Mr Searle's excellent photographs of the monster are too good to be true, the snake-like head and neck standing erect from the water like some plastic blow-up toy manufacturer's idea of a monster, the light and shade and weather on the loch inconsistent with the timing of the sightings he claims. Possibly there is an element of professional jealousy in some of these criticisms for there is another and less successful

monster-spotting organisation on the other side of the loch
– the official Loch Ness Investigation Bureau. The two
organisations do not seem to be drawn together by their
common purpose. Frank Searle says disparagingly that
the "other" investigators have had their grant withdrawn
because of their poor record of sightings. Certainly, it is
unimpressive compared with his own – about twenty-three
sightings and eighteen photographs during his five-year
vigil. Some people, say the other side, sourly, are born lucky.

But they are united in one respect: their scorn for the
Japanese venture to hunt the monster by submarine. This,
they say, was a farcical exercise in public relations by a race
who are concerned that their national image has become
over-serious and who wish to convince the world at large that
they are, au fond, a light-hearted, even a frolicsome people.
As visibility in the loch below twenty feet is nil, because of
the density of peat particles in the water, only a monster
so hell-bent on self-exposure that it actually rubbed noses
with the submarine would run much risk of detection by
this method.

Whatever his critics say about Mr Searle's photographs,
they look pretty convincing to most people. He obviously
relishes his position in local folk lore and is happy to talk to
his numerous visitors, at about 150 words a minute, about
the habits and history of the monster, while managing to
maintain the attitude that while you may be on holiday and
frivolously inclined to chat, he has a job of work to do. While
you question him he conveys the impression of a chancellor
on budget day, submitting tolerantly to interview with one
foot on the bottom step of Number 10 where other more
pressing, more important matters await him.

But perhaps he has become a little sensitive to criticism
over the last few months. Since our last visit, some of the
photographs have suddenly sprouted little labels giving the
names of witnesses to the sightings, young ladies most of
them, and mostly from faraway places with vague addresses
like New South Wales or Tucson, Arizona. However, his most

recent sighting, in July this year, was apparently witnessed by one Lynda Tate of Doncaster. Showing a nasty suspicious streak, I looked in his visitor's book and she wasn't there, possibly too overcome by the sight of the monster to sign her name. But it occurred to me that if she is alive and well and living in Doncaster, some GP must have her on his list. If he should happen to read this, he might ask her, on her next visit, if she was out on Loch Ness in a boat with Frank Searle at 5.25 a.m. on July 19 and if so, what happened. If the answer's printable, I'd love to know.

Visiting Frank Searle was a regular part of our Scottish holidays, despite the fact that in the early 1980s many of his photos were exposed as fakes and his reputation began to suffer. Then one summer in 1986 we found he had disappeared – to go treasure hunting on the West Coast it was rumoured, though no one seemed to know what particular treasure he was hunting. The truth, when it eventually emerged, was less romantic – he had moved to Fleetwood in Lancashire where he apparently lived a quiet and solitary life. Partially paralysed by a stroke in 1998 he spent his last years in a wheelchair and died in 2005, aged 84. Although all his photographs are now generally regarded as fakes, I think most people who met him thought that his belief in the monster was genuine. He was simply waiting for the right moment when he, his camera and the monster, would all coincide in time and space.

39

Anybody want a horse?

~

One of the advantages of dual citizenship is that you can carry on in one place in a way that might be frowned upon as eccentricity in another. Would it, for example, ever have occurred to us to ring up Air Traffic Control at Heathrow and ask if they'd mind diverting Concorde for a while because its flight path over our back garden was putting the guinea pigs off their greens? Probably not. But in Scotland it seemed natural enough to telephone the duty officer at Lossiemouth and tell him that the Hurricanes or MiGs or whatever they are that practise their low flying techniques over the loch were frightening the horse.

They frighten me, as a matter of fact, screeching past at hilltop level, black and sinister, sending the trout scurrying for cover. When I'm walking alone over the moor and they come at me like something out of Star Wars they seem so menacing and malevolent that it's hard to believe there's nothing personal in it. And I am of a fairly placid temperament, while the horse is more nervy, easily ruffled, unable to cope with stress, what an old fashioned textbook of psychiatry might term neurasthenic. No wonder she lays back her ears at the first sound of jets and bolts into the sunset.

I don't know why it's so tempting to anthropomorphise the horse. "She's so intelligent, sensitive, lovely with children, likes dogs," the previous owners told us. You'd have thought we wanted to employ it as a nanny. In fact it looked like any other horse to me: that is to say, shifty and a bit thick. Maybe that's unfair. It must be hard for a creature that can't look you straight in the eye not to look like a Mafioso.

But I am not the person to talk about horses. I never really took to them. Though goodness knows I tried hard enough at one time, when I was eleven and my best friend was going through a horsey phase. There are so many of life's varied activities that I have taken up so as not to lose face with someone whose good opinion I craved at the time. Some of them have become unexpected and lasting sources of pleasure, such as red wine, and water skiing and the French Impressionists, while others, like Mahler and piloting little aeroplanes and making pastry with wholemeal flour, have never really got off the ground, somehow. Riding horses was another; I feigned enthusiasm for a while, then settled for the same limited ambition as that (according to Jorrocks the comical, vulgar and ebullient character created by Robert Surtees in the mid 19th century) of Mr Bambado, riding master to the Doge of Venice – to add to the theory with as little practice as possible.

In fact, of course, we didn't ask Lossiemouth actually to stop the flights. That would have been unreasonably demanding. Scotland is still a form of Abroad after all, and, in spite of the fact that we pay rates here and have done for 20 years, man and boy, we still have the status of Holiday Visitor, which comes pretty low in the Highland pecking order. What we did was to ask them the approximate times of the fly pasts so that we could arrange for the horse to be riderless and confined to the garden, which is what we call the fenced off piece of moor immediately adjacent to the house, and not running free in the 600 acres beyond. And what *they* did was to say, well, how long are you going to be up here then? And when we said, for another three weeks, they said, ok, we won't fly over you at all for the next three weeks. Which raised my opinion of the RAF about 300%.

There must be techniques for catching horses in wide-open spaces – they must do it in Wyoming and places like that – but I suspect they involve two or three mounted cowboys and a lasso. The method we use ourselves employs a child on foot with a bridle and a handful of pony-nuts: it is time-consuming and not always successful. I suspect we lack the ruthlessness of the professional horse-handler. There are, for example, various non-Queensberry rules for getting an unwilling horse into a horsebox, such as passing a piece of barbed wire round its hindquarters and winching it forwards, which we have never been able to bring ourselves to use, in spite of the fact that the whole of the first and last day of every holiday is always spent devising more humane means of achieving the same end. That's something the previous owners never told us, that she suffers from claustrophobia, and it's not the sort of thing you can find out however much you run your hands over her fetlocks and count the rings in her teeth. But I can see their difficulty. "Out of London," as Jorrocks also said, "one can hardly get rid of an 'oss without more or less doing violence to one's feelings of integrity."

Which reminds me, my daughter's really outgrown her now, so would anyone in the Inverness area like to buy a 14.2 Palomino, Arab cross Connemara? Good jumper, lovely nature, just like one of the family. I was only joking about the claustrophobia.

A WOMAN'S PLACE?

40

There comes a tide in the affairs of woman

W
e are holed up for the next ten days or so, waiting for disaster. Last week burglars, this week floods; as for next week, *faites vos jeux*. All we can do is bite our fingernails, up the insurance and hide the matches.

I suppose the reason burglary is such a successful profession is (a) you know for sure they'll never do you because you've got nothing worth pinching; (b) if they *do* do you, they certainly won't choose today when you're only just nipping out to Sainsbury's for half an hour so it's hardly worth locking up properly; (c) if they do choose today, then they won't find your jewellery where you've cunningly hidden it, underneath the mattress or in your husband's socks.

Our burglars could have been a lot worse. There's some comfort to be found in being done over by real professionals – they may make off with your best goodies but they're such neat workers. The last lot were amateurs and left the place so ankle deep in debris that it was weeks before we discovered what was missing. Last week's stepped the drawers open methodically from the bottom and only threw out what they needed to get at the next layer. I came home before they'd really got under way, and it was such a pleasure to walk round the house finding the things they hadn't got round to, that we became almost complacent about the stuff they'd taken.

Consequently, we didn't discover the card table was gone till we tried to sit down at it to play bridge with my parents three nights later. "Didn't you notice it wasn't there when you tried to dust it?" said my mother, scandalised. Actually, the CID made more mess than the burglars. The fingerprint expert, a man of great devotion to duty, worked his way obsessionally round the house, even though he discovered from the first print that the cads had been wearing rubber gloves (my rubber gloves – they could at least have left those behind). "The powder will come off," he told me as he left, "if you tackle it straightaway with a damp cloth." This is not so. A damp cloth merely transforms a neat grey print into a splodgy grey smear and I think you should remember this if you ever have the same trouble. The correct way to deal with them is a jet of spray polish and a fierce rub with a duster. I must ring up the Brixton police and tell them this when I have a moment.

The flood, in a lot of ways, was more troublesome. It happened on a bad day. For one thing, the cat had just gone into labour and, for another, I had 34 pounds of strawberries lying about the kitchen, waiting to be dealt with. If I'd known that the cat was going into labour (she must have got her dates wrong – we were expecting them at the weekend), then I probably wouldn't have gone off picking strawberries but, as things turned out, it didn't matter at all because she got on with the job in hand in a manner which, for neatness and efficiency, would have been an example to the plumber.

I wouldn't have called the plumber if I had realised straightaway that it was drains I was dealing with and not just floods, because I always call the council for drains. Or, rather, I always have done ever since our first blocked drain when we first became householders and lived next door to a clever sort of chap who said if we had a garden rake and a bucket he'd show us how to unblock it ourselves. We didn't know him very well but he seemed to be the kind of man who liked showing you how to do things, so we stood round admiringly while he removed the manhole cover and lowered the garden rake. We watched in silence as he brought it up and shook the debris from the prongs into the bucket and, gradually, we realised that what he was bringing up on the prongs every time was French letters: dozens and dozens of them. We'd only lived there a couple of months and I was seven months' pregnant, so it was nothing to do with us, but the strange thing was that we'd always got the impression the couple we bought the house from didn't get on. Certainly, they'd had separate bedrooms but perhaps that had just added spice to their relationship. Somehow the situation tongue-tied us all, which was a pity because he must have known our predecessors better than we did, and, if we had speculated with him on the contents of the drain, he might have come up with an explanation more likely than the bizarre ones which later occurred to us.

Of course, if I hadn't picked the strawberries, I might not have discovered the flood (as I then thought it was), because it was only when I was carrying twenty or so pounds of them down to the deep freeze, leaving another ten or so pounds simmering into jam on the stove, that I discovered the cellar was ankle deep in water. It is always interesting to watch fate's warp and weft interweave to form life's rich tangled, etc, etc. It was not until I had gone through the Yellow Pages and telephoned a firm with the reassuring name Aqua Plumbing, and baled out the first two inches from the cellar, that some faint memory of an earlier flood, stirred perhaps by an even fainter smell of sewage, caused me to go into the garden and lift the manhole cover to find the main drain blocked.

I am surprised that I did not realise, earlier, that it might have been drains, as the previous occasion stuck in my memory for some time, because of the way the man from the council who came and dealt with it took to my daughter. There had been a similar flood, caused by the same blocked drain, and the man from the council had dealt with it quickly and capably with his rods and brushes. Finally, with a rushing mighty roar, the drain had emptied and the man from the council had leaned proudly over to survey his handiwork, causing the Biro in his top left hand breast pocket to fall out into the stinking depths below. Personally, I would have gone out and bought another Biro, but, because of some sentimental value it had for him, I forget what, the man from the council had preferred to climb down the shaft, on rungs still dripping, and retrieve the biro from a small pool which still remained at the bottom. Then he had climbed up again and, reasonably enough, asked if he might wash his hands.

Now, at that time, our youngest daughter was about three and had very fair curly hair of the sort that made adults sigh sentimentally and say "Ah, I wish I had one of your curls," and sometimes when they said this our elder daughter would lead her sister grimly by the hand from the room and return some minutes later brandishing a pair of scissors and a blond hank of hair, which she'd hand over to them. Later on, when they both realised that children in television commercials all have long straight hair, the elder one stopped being jealous and the younger one stopped simpering in a pleased way when anyone remarked on her curls, but glowered instead and grew her hair into plaits, so no one could see it was curly. Anyway, this drain man from the council walked all the way in through the hall, while I tried not to look at his boots, and then, while I was looking for some soap in the kitchen and he was waiting by the oven, this little blond three-year-old came and leaned up against him and looked up at him with large, appealing blue eyes and, absent-mindedly, as people used almost reflexively to do, he started running his hands through her curls. You can't say to people, not to people who've been kind enough to unblock your drains, "do you mind not running your filthy mitts through my daughter's hair," so I waited until he 'd washed his hands and left before I took her upstairs and shampooed it.

To get back to the man from Aqua Plumbing: he was a dainty man, although it seems wrong to describe a broad, middle aged plumber as dainty. It may have been his pink shirt and pale blue jeans, or the way his long, grey hair was tied back in a ribbon, buccaneerish fashion, or just the fact that he carefully drew on a pair of pink rubber gloves before he started work. Your real sewage expert, your drains man as-to-the-manner-born, seldom, I have noticed, wears gloves. But he seemed competent enough so I left him with his yards of rods, poking away with different attachments on the end, like a fisherman trying out different flies, and I went back to the jam. When I went out into the garden, some time later, the drain was still blocked and he was winching down the last of his rods. He was, he said, twenty feet out under the road and bringing up clay – and tree roots. If I asked him, the main sewer had caved in and it was a job for the council.

So I paid him and he gave me a receipt which said, truthfully enough, "For attempting to unblock main drain, £10," and then I telephoned the council and explained how my plumber had rodded out twenty feet under the main road and brought up clay and tree roots but my drain was still blocked for all that. The council came round at once and two young men with short hair, stripped to the waist, went straight down the manhole and unblocked the drain in a flash, while the third, a uniformed council employee, gave me a lecture about picking up strange plumbers from the Yellow Pages instead of calling the council straightaway. He also explained how there was a bend in our drain, just about where the drive joins the pavement, and how Aqua Plumbing's rods had failed to negotiate the bend but, instead, had drilled straight through the wall of the pipe and out under the main road. What I didn't tell him was that Aqua Plumbing had recommended that we had the whole of our pipe relined by a method involving liquid cement, plungers, springs and a couple of tractors. There are some situations you really can't expect the council to get you out of.

41

Role Reversal

Home comforts have deteriorated a bit round here
since I went back to work part time last spring, but
things took a definite upsurge during the week
before Christmas when my husband was at home for an
enforced convalescence. It was lovely to come home to a
blazing fire, my slippers warming, the children's fish fingers
bubbling away in the pan.

His first day home he decided to make bread. At 9.30 am
he rang me up at the office to ask where I kept the yeast.
Bottom shelf of the left hand cupboard nearest the sink, I told
him. Five minutes later he rang me again to say whereabouts
on the bottom shelf? About the middle, I said, somewhere
between the self-raising flour and the castor sugar. It wasn't,
he told me a few minutes later. Had I any other suggestions?
I said I knew perfectly well it was there, I'd seen it yesterday
and he'd better go and have another look and I'd hold on.
He was back pretty quickly this time, sounding reproachful.
He said I'd never mentioned it might be behind the tea.

At five minutes past ten he rang up to ask where the
poppy seeds were. I said what did he need poppy seeds for?

He said because his recipe said sprinkle with poppy seeds. I said yes, but in all the years I'd been making bread I'd never bothered to sprinkle with poppy seeds and it hadn't made any difference. He said he didn't think there was any point in doing these things if one didn't do them properly. So I said he could see if Mr Singh across the road at the Food Store had any, though I doubted it, but on no account was he to go to Mr Davidson at the dairy because Mr Davidson is terribly expensive and gives short change and is rude to old ladies and children but calls everybody sweetheart. Unfortunately, he also keeps a much better stock than nice Mr Singh, which is why there is always a little covey of locals outside his shop who have all sworn never to darken his doors again, collaring passing strangers to persuade them to go in and buy their bean sprouts or stuffed quails' eggs for them.

My husband rang up again at 10.20 to say that he'd decided to make herb bread, so while he was in Mr Davidson's buying the poppy seeds because Mr Singh hadn't got any he had bought thyme and tarragon and rosemary and parsley. I said I already had thyme and tarragon and rosemary and parsley, plenty of them, on the second shelf of the right hand cupboard nearest the oven; it was only poppy seeds I hadn't got because I didn't consider poppy seeds to be part of the well-run household's regular store-cupboard. I said I thought I was just going into an important meeting and it might be better if he didn't ring up again for a while.

In fact I didn't hear from him again for ages, so at about half past one I rang him. I said how was the bread going? He sounded exhausted. He said he hadn't managed to do a thing. As soon as he'd finished speaking to me last time my friend Bridget had dropped in to see me, but she'd been very pleased to see him even though I wasn't there, so he'd made coffee for them both and she had told him all about her friend Maurice who was an artist, but unfortunately an alcoholic as well and penniless to boot. It was getting very difficult for him to go on painting in his condition, partly because paints were so expensive and he couldn't afford them, but he'd led such an interesting life, being thrown out of boudoirs and into prisons on five continents, that Bridget thought he ought to write a book. The only trouble was that so much had happened to him it was difficult for him to know where to start. What did my husband think he ought to do? My husband said he thought Maurice should either start at the beginning and work his way through, sort of chronologically, or he could just pick out some particularly interesting incident and start there. Bridget said she thought that might be the best and she'd encourage him to start straight away. Did my husband think he might get on better if he (Maurice) got dried out first? My husband said that just then my friend Patricia from next door popped in but disappeared again when she found he had company. He sounded rather disappointed. He said before they'd really got their teeth into Maurice's alcoholism my friend Felicity appeared, so Bridget left. Felicity lives in Chiswick and is hardly ever around Herne Hill, so I was really sorry to miss her. My husband made another pot of coffee and caught up on about twelve months' gossip although he couldn't remember any of it. He said Felicity had just gone and he thought he had caffeine poisoning and could I get some more coffee on the way home because he'd run out. He asked however did I manage to work at home?

I told him that the only way to do it was to put the latch on the front door. Normally the door isn't locked so if people can push it open they assume you are at home. If you lock it they can't ring, because the bell doesn't work, so you don't have to pretend you can't hear them because you really can't. And, provided you close the kitchen door and work in the breakfast room, they can't see that you're in even if they bend down and peer through the letterbox. I said I thought he'd be well advised to adopt this plan of campaign if he was serious about wanting to be left alone with his dough, because once the word got around that it was him in residence and not me he'd find himself with a regular outpatient clinic. Not that we're a neurotic lot in Herne Hill, but everybody has their little problems.

I found it rather annoying that his bread, once he'd finished it twenty-four hours later, was actually much better than mine. By the end of the week he had mastered plaited loaves and was into muffins and Italian bread sticks, and talking about nourishing his yeast on molasses and honey as though it was a dear but delicate relation. It's a good thing he went back to work before he'd raised the rest of the housewifely arts to an equally unattainable level.

42

Keeping the GP at bay

~

Publishers are canny people. It is no wonder, such is the public's preoccupation with health, that they have hit on an area in which they can corner both ends of the market. Give the public a health guide and you are satisfying not only the ones who are keen to stay healthy, but also those who need to prove they have a perfectly adequate reason for feeling under the weather.

For the past three years I have been working on one of those family health guides and can vouch for the fascination that they hold for others. And, while I would be the first to admit that the job is no substitute for six years in medical school and a couple of house jobs, it is an excellent way to gain medical charisma.

Work companions soon took to drifting upstairs to consult us about things they weren't sure they should bother their doctor with, and we'd knock off the editing and coffee-drinking and clear up many a little problem that might otherwise have cluttered up their GP's day.

Actually, I found these morning surgeries useful because part of the book was devoted to a series of self-diagnosis symptom charts. Although these were all being tested in the field by a band of cooperative GPs, I found it reassuring to conduct a few spot checks of my own. I had relied heavily on Barry for help with these. Barry was our resident hypochondriac and we knew it could only be a matter of days before he took time off from his own GP to give us a whirl.

At first he seemed reluctant to do what was expected of him – he knew his own reputation as well as we did – and he'd just pause in the doorway on his way upstairs, ostensibly to discuss who was going down to the pub at lunch-time or other cultural matters. Then, one day, in an off-hand sort of way, he said. "Those charts. I'd like to have a look at them."

"What are you complaining of?" I said.

"Tell me what you've got," said Barry.

"Cough," I said, "constipation, runny nose ..."

He shook his head, so I offered him toothache, headache, noises in the ear and halitosis, but he wasn't interested.

The last thing you want to do with a hypochondriac is pander to his sense of the dramatic, but after a while I ran out of trivial symptoms and was onto the hard stuff – things like swollen abdomen, recurrent vomiting and blurred vision. When I got to pain in the chest his eyes lit up.

"I'll have that one," he said. He worked his way slowly through the chart until he came to the last box, which read, 'Your pain is probably caused by anxiety and is no cause for concern.'

Barry looked outraged and I chalked it up as yet another success for the charts. It was obviously a good learning experience, too, because the next day he was back again demanding another go. This time he was more specific about the pain – it came on when he exercised and disappeared at rest. Sometimes it radiated down his left arm. He was well pleased with his new diagnosis. "I told you it wasn't anxiety," he said with quiet satisfaction.

You'd be quite wrong if you thought he then went off to badger his proper doctor. Barry wasn't interested in treatment. He simply wanted some acknowledgment that he was, as he had long suspected, in pretty poor shape. He went contentedly about his work for several days, pausing occasionally to clasp a protective hand rather far too far to the left of his breastbone.

The office hysteric, Nadia, demanded a slightly different approach. Nadia had once auditioned for, but failed to get, the leading part in a subsequently very successful stage musical. She was unable to forget, or let anyone else forget, this non-event and had ever since gone singing about her work in a voice which was undoubtedly powerful enough to penetrate the furthest reaches of Drury Lane, but which seemed a bit over the top in the confines of our small and overcrowded premises.

Nadia's speciality was abdominal pain, which struck whenever two or three were gathered together to form an audience but seldom, worse luck, scythed her down in mid-song. Doubled up she would stagger into the office and lie prone (or is it supine – at any rate face upwards) on the floor while we prodded her gingerly and said 'does this hurt?' Nadia's pain was vague and shifting and gave us no diagnostic satisfaction. Prod where we might, there was no board-like rigidity which could have indicated an acute abdomen or acute tenderness at McBurney's point. Neither would she admit to any less glamorous symptoms such as diarrhoea, which could have enabled us to diagnose one of those common things that commonly occur.

I know what you're thinking: you can't muck around with abdominal pain, that we should have passed her on to a professional. You misunderstand. We were the last refuge of the medically misunderstood. And, while we may have been abysmally ignorant about abdominal pain, we had a sound knowledge of the patient. Nadia wasn't interested in the diagnosis, only the examination. Nadia undiagnosed was centre stage. If we'd actually found something wrong we'd have lost interest and she would have had to think of the next act.

After a while, we got a bit above ourselves and started making diagnoses on people who hadn't even asked for them. We were convinced, for a time, that one of the directors had diabetes. I can't remember exactly why – all publishers suffer from excessive thirst, his was not unusual – except he was a bit skinny and had boils.

We debated whether we should ask him for a urine sample or simply tell him he looked run down and advise him to see a doctor. Luckily we'd finished the book before we'd lost touch with reality enough to do either.

43

If you can't stand the heat
Get back in the kitchen

All over the western world, if one is to believe everything one reads, women are popping out like butterflies from the grey chrysalis of domesticity, emerging to shake their rumpled wings in a brighter, more colourful existence. Freedom, it's called, and liberation: fine words and a fine cause, but nothing much to do with the working life of the working wife. I suppose it's freedom to be able to lock the door behind you in the morning, climb onto a bus and, for a mere 26p, be swept away to another four walls, another desk wrist-deep in paper; but it doesn't always feel like it. The poor old working wife misses out on the perks all round. She can't take the morning off to go strawberry picking or the afternoon off to watch Wimbledon; she has to go to Sainsbury's on a Saturday morning and do the ironing in the middle of the night. If she's part time it's always the wrong part – she isn't at home when the hamster dies and she isn't at work for the celebration booze-up after the Frankfurt Book Fair. "Christopher keeps a bottle of whisky in his bottom drawer," I was told fairly early on. "He

brings it out if you go along after 6 pm with any problems."
But, as my biggest problem was getting away by 5 pm, I
never got a sniff of it. We do it for the money, of course,
but that sometimes seems a rather crude reason so let us
wrap it up a little. Mental stimulation – how about that?
Mothers left to mind small children turn into cabbages:
everybody knows that.

No wonder we resent the gay laughing butterflies,
prancing about outside. But once we get back to work (or so
the story goes) we can keep the fires of our intellect ablaze
with scintillating conversation, meet fascinating new people
and thrash out the world's problems over the morning coffee
break. Well, I don't know about your office, but I do know
that ours was a very jolly place where the football results
and last night's television and this morning's office gossip
had star billing in the conversation and thrashing out the
world's problems had a very low priority indeed. The place
for stimulating conversation is over coffee with your non-
working mates who know that the Bad Fairy of Hearth and
Home (who wears a saucepan on her head and has crossed
nappy pins atop her wand) is lurking to catch them off their
guard and turn them into vegetables. They conscientiously
read *The Guardian* and *New Statesman* and *Private Eye* to
keep her at bay and are only too eager to discuss the world's
problems as a welcome bit of light relief from their own.

What else are we looking for? Power? Responsibility?
There's usually more of that around in the unpaid, voluntary
jobs that women get up to before they go back to "real"
work. Job satisfaction? After years of doing your own thing,
running your own show, it is not always easy, let alone
satisfying, to accept a bit part in somebody else's. The newly
working wife may have to grit her teeth a good many times
to avoid becoming not only bossy but also insubordinate.
It used to take four people three weeks at work to arrive at
a decision, and then top management usually reversed it
next day. Think of all the decisions we have to make before
breakfast. Long term planning decisions, such as shall I

take sausages or fish fingers out of the freezer for tea? Or quick, snap judgments such as is it going to rain and should my son take his anorak? And short term policy decisions such as what should the middle child do if her Best Friend who turned nasty yesterday won't walk to school with her this morning?

It is difficult for the working wife to feel really liberated in the morning with all the bits of family administration that have to be done before she can actually get out and become free. Finding things – one bathing cap, one pair husband's spectacles, three lots lunch money, extra money for school photos (daughter looks delightful, says it's *ghastly*, I look *awful*, you're not to buy any; son looks as though he has auditioned successfully for part of *Just William*, studies them like Narcissus, wants the lot). Find Latin homework, small piebald felt horse without which elder daughter will undoubtedly fail chemistry exam; letter from school with tear-off slip to say will/will not help at jumble sale; pencil to fill in tear-off slip; more decisions about will/ will not help at jumble sale. Remind eldest to feed cats, second to feed rabbit, youngest to feed guinea pig; tell all to make own beds. Feed cats, rabbit, guinea pig and make beds. Find old white sheet to make ghost costume for 4A's assembly play; say good gracious, you don't need me to make that – all you need to do is cut out a couple of holes. Make ghost costume. Convince middle child that slight ache in left index finger need not mean No Swimming. Remember, Wednesday is cleaning lady's day. Leave key with neighbour, ring up cleaning lady to say where key is, write note to cleaning lady telling her what to clean and find money for cleaning lady. No change. Write another note to cleaning lady saying please buy loaf bread with £5 note and take money out of change. Tidy kitchen, breakfast room, hall, sitting room so cleaning lady can actually clean. Leave sandwiches and chocolate biscuits for children to alleviate guilt at not being there when they come home from school. Arrive at work early to alleviate guilt at having to leave early. Watch others arrive, munching cheese rolls because they got up too late to have breakfast.

Working away from home destroys a few illusions. First, that without me in it to keep order the home would rapidly degenerate into a first-class slum. Or (an alternative, less charitable view), the reason our home is a first-class slum is that my Canute-like efforts are powerless to stem the tidal wave of devastation caused by the rest of the family's slip-shod habits. Wrong, and wrong again; the house stays a whole lot tidier when I am out of it. I find that difficult to understand.

Second, in my staying-at-home days I had these fleeting moments when I regarded my husband as a social wet blanket, wanting only a quiet evening with his feet up while I was justifiably hopping up and down, anxious to get out and meet people and do things. Nowadays anyone who comes home and groans, "Oh God, do we have to go," has my entire sympathy.

As for me, I have tasted freedom and it has worn me out. I'm taking a break now so if you'll excuse me for a moment I'll climb out of my strait-jacket of liberation and crawl back into my cocoon.

My daughters assure me that here and now, 50 years on, the problems for the working mother haven't changed much!

FRIENDS AND NEIGHBOURS

44

Bomb Alert

Mr Pastorelli, taking his dog for its customary evening stroll around Herne Hill, called in to say did we know we had a couple of unattended bags or packages sitting in our drive. There's a lot of intuitive appeal in that kind of dramatic situation, like the possibility of being hi-jacked whenever you get into an aeroplane, which is why I always look around hopefully at the other passengers to see if any of them are disguised Arabs with sand on their boots.

I followed Mr Pastorelli into the garden and he showed me the bag, which was a shabby old brown leather handbag, and the package, which was a tatty plastic holdall. They were tucked under the back of the car, just where you'd imagine they would be tucked if they were the sort of thing we were wondering if they might be, though whether Mr Pastorelli and I would have recognised that unless it was black, spherical, smoking, and labelled "BOMB" is another matter. Mr Pastorelli said you had to admit they looked pretty suspicious if you had a suspicious sort of mind, and who hadn't nowadays? And I said yes, but surely there was a perfectly innocent explanation if we could only think of it because, on the whole, the IRA operated more widely in Mayfair than in Herne Hill, on account of the publicity being better if you got a better class of victim. Mr P said down by the station every other house had an Irishman in it and looked like a bomb factory, and I said that might be so, but I didn't think I had, even inadvertently, done anything to offend any of them. Then Mr Pastorelli said persuasively was I absolutely sure they weren't mine, as though there were a faint chance I was suffering from amnesia and might be prodded into recollection.

One thing, which puzzled me, I said, was the fact that there were two of them: a bag and a package. So far as I could make out, the IRA was not so flush with gelignite that they could afford to flash their bombs around in pairs. Perhaps they wanted to make doubly sure, said Mr Pastorelli, ho, ho. Actually, I was feeling a bit hurt by now. Once the initial excitement had worn off, it wasn't very nice to think that anyone was getting at us to that extent. Probably just a case of mistaken identity, said Mr P comfortingly, but I said that all the really important people in the area, the politicians and the editor of the BMJ and the organisers of the Miss World Contest, lived a mile away down the hill in Dulwich and I didn't think even the IRA could get it that wrong.

By now we were both beginning to think that decisive action was called for on somebody's part, probably mine as the bomb was kind of in our court. Left to myself I might, having an ostrich-like nature, have gone to bed and hoped that the trouble might vanish overnight. I mean, you used to be able to leave an unattended bag or package lying around Herne Hill and absolutely rely on its being gone in the morning, but nowadays people are more careful what they swipe. Or I might just have waited till my husband came home and pointed out that anything with wires in it was his responsibility. But just then Mr Pastorelli's dog, beset by none of our inhibitions about appearing either cowardly or foolhardy, strolled nonchalantly forwards and nosed open the plastic hold-all. As one, Mr Pastorelli and I leaped backwards into the rose bushes, but, as there was no immediate explosion, we edged out again and approached the dog, who was standing quite placidly beside the bag, eating an unidentified object which, on closer inspection, proved to be a luncheon-meat sandwich, rather curled at the edges. Gingerly, I peered into the holdall but its contents looked more unappetising than threatening – some more sandwiches, assorted grubby hankies and paper bags, a tin of pilchards, a disintegrating cream doughnut. Emboldened, Mr P stretched out one hand to open the handbag, leaning back and covering his eyes with the other, so that even if he were to lose the tips of his fingers he might escape being blinded by the blast.

The handbag contained an old age pensioner's bus pass in the name of Maudie Stevens, and a pair of minute, child-sized spectacles, inexplicably wrapped up with another doughnut and covered with cream. There was a first world war wedding photograph of a tiny Edwardian bride and a uniformed groom, and several sheets of folded paper with the owner's name written waveringly, over and over again, "I am Maudie Stevens", as though needing reassurance of her own identity. There was also a telephone number printed large on the lining – RING 748 3933. So I thanked Mr Pastorelli and said I thought I could handle things now, and gave the rest of the luncheon-meat sandwiches to the dog and put the children back to bed because by this time they were gathered on the doorstep, over-dramatising things as usual and refusing to let me bring the handbag into the house in case Mr P and I had overlooked some high explosive in a corner.

Then I rang 748 3933, like the handbag said. A woman answered and I said I was wondering if she had lost her handbag because I seemed to have found it. And she, rather uninterestedly, as though this sort of thing was always happening (as indeed it evidently was), said oh well, no, it wasn't hers, it would be her mother-in-law's. She said her mother-in-law was very old and inclined to wander and she, the daughter-in-law, had said she wasn't fit to be let out of hospital this last time and this just showed how right she'd been. It turned out that the old lady had wandered all the way from Hounslow before depositing her belongings in our garden, but it was difficult to see how she could go much further with no money and no bus pass and not even a cream doughnut to sustain her. So I said should I ring the police and ask them to look out for her, and the daughter-in-law said she supposed that would be the best thing, and her mother-in-law would be easy to recognise because she was a very small woman, really very small indeed, and would be wearing a fur coat that looked as old as she was. So then I rang the Brixton police and said would they mind looking out for a small old lady in a fur coat who was wandering around somewhere in the Herne Hill area. And the policeman at the other end said was I reporting a missing person then? And I said, not missing exactly, because we knew whereabouts she was, just wandering and a long way from home and without even a bus pass. But the policeman said unless she was reported officially missing by the relatives it wasn't up to them to take any action. And I said maybe not but it didn't sound to me as though the relatives were missing her at all, far from it, and surely they could just cruise around and pick her up and make sure she was all right, because she'd be easy to spot, being so small and fur-coated and carrying nothing at all. In the end he said very ungraciously he'd tell the patrol cars to look out for her, but I think that was just to get me off the line.

The next day the old lady's son rang up to tell me his mother had eventually ended up in Clapham and was now safely back in hospital. He said the policeman in Clapham had been most unhelpful and wouldn't even lend her the money to go home in a taxi, so he'd had to come off his night shift and go home to meet her and pay the fare. I said the Brixton police had been much the same, although usually they're very pleasant down at the nick and once even had an Open Day and let the children stroke their horse. I told him about the bomb scare and we agreed that they didn't know their own luck that night, just dealing with a lost little old lady in a fur coat when it might have been something really nasty, like 10lbs of gelignite.

Were Mr Pastorelli and I being paranoid? Maybe a bit – but remember that the 1970s were the most intense period of IRA activity in Britain; unaccompanied packages were automatically regarded as suspicious. Though admittedly Herne Hill wasn't really high profile enough to be a likely target.

45

A stroll down doppelganger lane

~

I used to think the New York grid system was an unimaginative way of naming city streets and that 146 East 93rd Street was a pretty soulless sort of address. I know better now. You know exactly where you are with East 93rd Street and, what's more, so does everyone else. Let us suppose, for example, for within these columns all things are possible, that you have managed to acquire, at an amazingly modest price, a desirable residence in York Road, SE1, somewhere between Lambeth Palace and St Thomas's Hospital. Excitedly you send out your little change of address cards, unaware that within the Metropolitan area are no less than 24 other York Roads, four York Avenues, a York Buildings, two York Closes, York Gates, and York Places, three York Ways, and York Hill, House, Rise, and Square. It should be apparent to you that there are possibilities for error within the system.

In our own small corner, over the last few years, we have built up a dossier of confusion that should persuade any reasonable Council that something needs to be done about its street nomenclature. The house at 42 Herne Hill Road is a larger, seedier version of our own at 42 Herne Hill, and, judging by the variety of their post, which appears on our breakfast table each morning, more people live there. I can tell you exactly how many, as a matter of fact, because on Gas Conversion Day last week a man from the Gas Board appeared to look at my check-meters. What are they? I asked. Do I have any? "They're the money-in-the-slot ones," he said, looking at his list "and yes, you've got ten." I took him around a bit to convince him I hadn't and then sent him round to Herne Hill Road.

This sort of thing happens every day. It is our alter ego, that house and its occupants, and sometimes I'm not quite sure where they begin and I end. It's like leading several different lives all at once, and some of them are quite exciting.

One day I answered the door to a small, shabby-looking fellow, wearing a fawn raincoat and matching woolly gloves. He was evasive when asked his business but eventually produced a tatty envelope from somewhere in the depths of the raincoat and extracted from it a sheet of paper to which was attached a photograph. He tried ineffectually to hide the letter heading with a woolly glove but I could see that it was something like Acme Investigation Agency. The photograph was of a wedding group, the bride a large, plain, rather formidable-looking girl, gift-wrapped in many layers of tulle, the groom several sizes smaller and already with a look of evident regret upon his face.

"Have you seen *him*," demanded the man, dabbing a finger at the groom, "going in *there*?" and he nodded surreptitiously in the direction of number 40, next door. "Or," he added, "coming out?"

Now, although it was not surprising that the gentleman in the photograph was finding consolation elsewhere, I thought it was unlikely to be in that particular quarter. The lady at number 40 at that time was delightful, but highly respectable and not a day under 75. I explained this as well as I could, but didn't tell him that he might have better luck at 42 Herne Hill Road, partly out of a sneaking sympathy for his quarry and partly from a feeling that he was, after all, meant to be a detective and somebody didn't seem to be getting their money's worth. He went off down the path and I watched him through the hole in the front door glass where the burglars broke in. He stood for a while forlornly on the pavement, a slight, disconsolate figure, beating his woolly gloves together against the cold, looking up and down the road, wondering, perhaps, what Perry Mason would have done in similar circumstances. After a while, he turned and came up the garden path again and knocked at the door. "Can you tell me," he said, "which way the buses go back into Town?"

They're a very mixed bag at number 42 – the other 42, that is. There's Mr Lipmann, who's taking an Open University course; I can't think that he ever manages to get his essays in on time, with all the toing and froing of post that goes on. Then there was Beverley O'Grady, who made a down payment on a Singer sewing machine back in 1970 and then did a flit, taking it with her. For two years we forwarded all the demands from Singers, writing "Try Herne Hill Road" on the envelope, and they all came back with "Not Known Here" all over them. When Singers started threatening to take us, or rather Beverley, to court, we wrote them a long letter explaining the situation and we haven't heard from them since. I expect Beverley's gone to ground in the Falls Road, sewing uniforms for the IRA.

Mr Benjamin is my favourite and he's probably the oldest inhabitant, too. At any rate, he's been there as long as we have. Incidentally, Mr Benjamin, if you're reading this – and I hope you're not – I'd like to explain about one or two air letters you never got from your brother in Jamaica. The trouble is that air letters, being so light, sometimes get caught in a strange down-draft of air from the letterbox and may float sideways under the chest instead of dropping straight down onto the mat. When the guinea pig escapes, he hides under there and chews paper, so, by the time I found them, they hardly seemed worth forwarding. I feel bad about it though.

Some of the things they've tried to deliver to us would have been quite useful, like the builder's skip and the carpet, but unfortunately I was out when the man came to deliver the wood, and the lorry was just about to drive off when I got back. The piece of hardboard it had brought was leaning against the house. It was about 12 feet by six and was partly obscuring the dining room window. I flagged the lorry down. "I didn't order it, you know," I told the driver. Now you try telling a lorry driver, at 5.30 on a wet Friday afternoon, that you didn't order the wood he has to get rid of before he goes home, when he has a piece of paper proving that you did. "It says 42, dunnit?" he snarled, thrusting the delivery note under my nose, "It says Herne Hill, dunnit? Whaddya mean, you don't want it?" It stayed there for some days, presumably till whoever it was round at Herne Hill Road who wanted to make cupboards rang up the wood yard saying, "What about my wood?"

But there are changes on the horizon, and the thought saddens me. The other day I found an estate agent in the hall, looking at the cracks in the ceiling and making notes.

"The door was open," he said, "so I came in and got started. Hope you don't mind."

He was aggrieved when I said I did. "Madam," he said, as though explaining a simple point to a young, rather awkward child, "Madam, if you won't let me look around, I can't give you a proper valuation. Now can I?" He didn't believe me when I said I didn't want to sell the place. He had a piece of paper, too, and he knew that I did.

I hope it's not the end of the road for Mr Lipmann and Mr Benjamin and Mr Robins whose girlfriend sends him such very affectionate postcards every time she goes on holiday, and Miss Driscoll who never renews her television licence. I hope they don't sell the house and take out all the check-meters and put a dull old family in. But if they do, I hope, when they're clearing the place out, they keep a look out for six years' accumulation of letters addressed to us. I know for a fact that my brother sent us a postcard from Monte Carlo in 1968, which never arrived. They've never forwarded it. Or anything else, for that matter.

46

Don't rock the boat

There's always someone worse off than you, which is what all those people who say it's a funny old world also say. So I always feel sorry for people in supermarkets who live such solitary lives that they see the week through on a tin of pilchards and a couple of packets of chocolate digestives. And if they've any sense they feel sorry for me with my two loaded trolleys and a bill long enough to welcome an American hero home all on its own.

It is a universal drive, this urge to prove that someone else is at the tail end of the pecking order. Perhaps that's why it's so disturbing to come across people who don't know when they are badly off. "How's Sophie?" I asked my friend Maureen the other day. Sophie is a mutual friend who has just had a breast removed. "Terrible, I'm really worried about her," said Maureen, worriedly. Maureen's a social worker. "She's acting as if everything's fine. I can't get her to express any negative feelings about it at all." Maureen was once drummed out of a ward by an indignant Sister for reducing a patient to tears. The patient had had a miscarriage and Maureen felt that her mourning reaction wasn't getting under way quickly enough so she helped it along. Just to provoke her I told her a story I'd heard about a woman who had reached the age of 40 without acquiring husband, lover or children and with no immediate prospect of any of them. So she had a prophylactic double mastectomy. No breast cancer risk. No bras. No negative feelings.

We have a neighbour who is the epitome of the brave little woman. Madge has a peptic ulcer, angina and chronic bronchitis and every winter since 1972 we've been convinced would be Madge's last, but it never has been. The reason Madge has kept going so well is simply that her husband Cecil is so much worse off than she is. Cecil (so Madge has at one time or another told the whole neighbourhood in the strictest confidence) suffered various ill-defined but debilitating injuries in the last war, which have accounted for his being a) off work and b) impotent ever since.

They were also responsible – and here public sympathy for Cecil was unanimous – for his glass left eye. Cecil's familiar figure could be seen every Monday, Tuesday, Wednesday and Thursday mornings striding down the hill to the betting shop and, in spite of the black patch he wore continually over his left eye, you could always be sure of a cheery wave of recognition from the other side of the road. Doesn't he manage well, we all said? On Fridays he went to the market with Madge to help her carry back the shopping, on account of her dicky heart. Madge seldom went out on her own, because Cecil needed her. Cecil managed to keep going somehow, because of Madge. "How are you Cecil?" you'd say when you met in the street. "Not too bad, not too bad, mustn't grumble," he'd say bravely. "I can't let things get me down; it wouldn't be fair on Madge." "And how's Madge?" you'd ask then. "Marvellous," he'd say enthusiastically. "She's marvellous to me. Nobody ever had a better wife. She's up a ladder now polishing the picture rails, would you believe it. I don't know what I'd do without her. Her heart's not too good this week though." As a marriage it wasn't everybody's idea of an idyll but it obviously suited them.

The hospital responsible for Cecil and Madge's ongoing medical care was a centre of excellence, which, in case it might prefer to remain anonymous, I shall call Queens. They kept Cecil ticking over very nicely until soon after their Golden Wedding when Madge's ulcer blew up and she had to spend a couple of weeks in Queens. Cecil coped very well all the time Madge was in, cooking himself proper meals and remembering to take the dog for a walk, but as soon as she came home again he became depressed enough for us to suggest that he attended the out-patient department of another centre of excellence, the psychiatric hospital just across the road from Queens. Naturally enough, hearing that Cecil was under Queens they sent across the road for his notes, which included the information that his central nervous system was intact except for his glass left eye. "Poor old chap," they said, "no wonder he gets a bit low now and then". In fact, he got worse and was admitted, and a keen young Registrar who hadn't seen his notes did a full physical examination and came up with the fact that Cecil had 6/6 vision in both eyes. That's impossible, said the consultant. The left one's glass. Go and do it again. So he did and the result was the same.

At the next ward round Cecil's patch was removed and, after some persuasion, he admitted to a hazy perception of light with his left eye. "Splendid," said the consultant, clapping a hand over the other eye. "Now try to read that card." Cecil said it looked very murky but he managed to decipher it eventually.

The curing of Cecil's glass eye was a nine-day sensation in the neighbourhood but the repercussions on the dynamics of Madge and Cecil's marriage lasted a lot longer than that. Madge's caring attitude to Cecil vanished overnight. Hostile cries of "Bloody well do it yourself," rang around their flat and Cecil, deprived of the sympathy and solicitude, which had been his in such large measure for so long, got more and more depressed. And Madge, after years of fortitude, diverted the care and attention she'd previously given to

Cecil's ill health to her own. For the next couple of years, as soon as one of them came out of hospital, the other went in.

Maureen did what she could, but even she had to admit that Madge needed very little help in learning to express the pent-up negative feelings of 50 years. However, like most long-established couples they had their own unorthodox ways of working out their problems. After a while, Cecil was seen about with the black patch once more firmly established over his left eye and gradually things returned to normal. It was just as well that the hospital didn't muck about trying to cure his impotence as well. Rocking the boat is one thing, but I'm afraid that might have sent the marriage right to the bottom.

47

Naming the product

~

Every now and then my friend Brenda rings me up to ask if I know nine men in the 35 to 45 age bracket, Registrar-General's Class III, over 6 foot, who wash every day with Palmolive but never touch underarm deodorant or aftershave. Sometimes they have to wear Van Heusen shirts as well, or take package holidays on the Costa del Sol, or have their mothers-in-law living with them on amicable terms. One of the things Brenda does for a living – and there are plenty of others but they do not involve such tight job specifications – is to organise groups of consumers for market researchers to beaver away at. I thought it sounded like money for old rope when she first told me about it, but then she said her first assignment was to collect nine full time working women with at least 2.5 children under 10 who cooked by gas and cleaned out their ovens every week and I realised things were tougher than they seemed.

Brenda's quest to uncover pockets of uniformity within the fascinating diversity of mankind has led her into some dodgy situations, such as loitering outside all the Brixton pubs at closing time at the height of the Troubles and begging those of the emerging clientele sober enough to speak to tell her whether they'd spent the evening drinking Young's bitter in pints. Because she's an ex-actress, is tall and beautiful, and is always accompanied by a soppy English setter called James, she gets a better response than one might expect. The following Tuesday evening at 8 p.m. her sitting room was packed with nine Irish pint-drinkers under the age of 35, all apparently happy to give up an evening's drinking for coffee and biscuits and the three quid each, which the market researcher doles out at the end of the session.

I had my first turn the other day. She has to be careful with her friends, because members of the group aren't supposed to know each other, which is difficult in a place like Herne Hill, although if you keep "knowing each other" to a strict, almost biblical sense and don't count having seen each other in Tesco's or being on nodding terms at PTA meetings it's perfectly possible. Of course, we'd all be prepared never to have seen each other in our lives if it would help Brenda over a difficult patch, but she's so honest she won't have it. Even over the hand washing she had a tussle with her conscience. I fitted almost perfectly into her sample (nine women with automatic washing machines who never used Stergene and did a hand-wash at least once a week), but there was a bit of a problem. For one thing, I have had a deprived adulthood with none of the sexy Janet Reger underwear that cannot be bunged into the washing machine. For another, those silk shirts and woolly jerseys that haven't already been ruined by the washing machine, lie around like sludge in the bottom of the laundry basket for weeks until the indignation of their owners overcomes my natural resistance to hand-washing. I do get around to it eventually, I explained, but to say it was at least once a week was stretching it a bit. Poor Brenda was about to delete me from her list and cast around for another sucker when I realised that if you counted holidays in Scotland, when I have no machine and wash by hand practically every day, or that's what it feels like, then over the year that would easily push my average up to the weekly mark.

So at eight o'clock on Tuesday I joined the rest of the sample at Brenda's. James, who gets over-excited when there's company, drooled over each of us in turn and filched biscuits from the coffee table, while the market researcher fixed up a little video machine in the corner. She was going to show us a film, she told us, which was an idea for a television advertisement, and we had to watch it very carefully and then she'd ask us some questions about it. She said we could say anything we wanted about the film because she was from a quite independent company not associated with the product at all, and no one's feelings were going to be hurt. So we all sat slightly forward on the sofa and watched this rather manic-looking woman performing a sort of mime, while excited off-stage voices tried to guess what it was she was miming, in the manner of some television game, which I had neither seen nor heard of. Naturally, the off-stage voices got it in the end, but none of us did, in spite of the fact that the name of the product, and indeed a picture of it, had apparently been flashed onto one side of the screen halfway through as a help for viewers at home. She showed us the film four times and, at the end of the fourth time, a woman in the corner said she still hadn't got the name of the product and she thought it was all those disembodied yapping voices that were putting her off. Personally, she thought a bit of nice music, like in the Hovis ad, would be better, so that even if you couldn't catch on to what they were meant to be advertising, at least it was a pleasure listening to it. "Oh dear," said the market researcher, "what else did the film make us feel?" Most of us said it made us feel as if now would be a good time to go out and put the kettle on. We also said that although you could afford to play guessing games with the public if you were Guinness or Schweppes, it was a bit pretentious to assume you were a household word when half the group had started the evening thinking you were a lavatory cleaner and the other half thought you were either a washing-up liquid or something for cleaning dentures.

What none of us realised was that the product was meant to be all soft and bubbly and gentle with delicate things, and that softness and bubbliness and gentleness were what the manic woman in the film was trying to convey. And we said that her fingernails were far too long. Anything else, said the market researcher? So then I told her that there was probably nothing wrong with the product that a change of name wouldn't put right and had they thought of trading it with a drug company? It seemed to me that Stergene would be a very good name for a fertility pill while on the other hand something like Librium had all the qualities of softness etc., etc., that might be needed to care for Janet Reger underwear. But the market researcher said market research wasn't meant to originate fundamental changes, only to make sure the image was right. "Did that mean," we all said, a bit indignant, "that our evening's work had all been for nothing? Apart from the three quid?" "Not really," said the market researcher. "They'll probably take the point about the fingernails."

TRAVEL ENRICHES THE MIND

48

Le Camping

~

*P*erhaps this piece should be re-titled 'Plus ça change.' This time round I am a passionate Remainer but, reading this piece again, I see that my reasons for wanting to remain in the EU now are pretty much the same as my reasons for wanting to remain out of it then.

There have been murmurings from Brussels, I gather, about our television programmes; they do not conform to Common Market standards (too many repeats). Murmurings, too, about our tomato production, which is embarrassingly good by comparison with EEC standards. I haven't got a lot to say in favour of British television but I do like repeats because I always miss things first time round – in fact I've just missed *The Forsyte Saga* for the third time because it seemed so immoral to watch television in the afternoons. And I like tomatoes, too.

This may sound as though I'm anti-Common Market, but I'm not. I'm not particularly for it, either. In fact I cannot help feeling that it is a difficult and complex issue which even the members of the cabinet, who must be more intelligent and better informed than I am, cannot agree upon. That is one of the reasons – in fact, come to think of it it's more or less the only reason – that I like to elect a government; they can make these difficult decisions for me and if Harold Wilson calls a referendum on the issue, he is evading his responsibilities and I shall spoil my ballot paper by writing a note on it telling him so. The only reason he wants one is so that when things go from worse to dreadful, as they are bound to do, he can point out that it is all our fault.

All this has brought me some way from where I wanted to be, which is talking about camping. For where, asks the niggling anti-marketeer in the back of my mind, is this imposition of European standards on our British way of life going to stop? Some of you, perhaps through advancing age or Grade A distinction awards, may have neither the need nor the inclination to go camping, but I can assure you that it's no longer just a matter of rubbing two sticks together beneath the stars. Camping has gone a long way and nowhere has it gone further than on the far side of the Channel. Any estate agent would be proud to have on his books some of the tents we saw when we were camping down through France last year. We have a tent, too, but it doesn't look like theirs. In fact we have two tents: one is a small, traditionally tent-shaped tent, which so shamed us beside all the two-up, two-down variety, which we met on the continental camp sites, that we invested, this year, in a friend's cast off tent of the frame variety, so as not to let the side down next time we went. It took us a long time, practising in the garden, to get it right, mostly because we assumed it was an endoskeletal tent, whereas three hours' hard work eventually proved that it was exoskeletal, with the canvas suspended from the frame by a series of hooks and rubber rings. "Now try it in a force 8 gale," said our next-door neighbour, who had watched the process interestedly over the fence, offering destructive advice. It reminds me, that tent, of a story in one of the children's books, called The Saggy Baggy Elephant, and once they start imposing Minimum Camping Standards, we won't be allowed past the gate.

Do you know what French girls wear when they're camping? They wear crisply ironed shirts and white pleated skirts and their toenails are painted and when you meet them in the washroom, trying to get the worst of the Mediterranean out of your hair, they are applying a full Helena Rubinstein *maquillage*. French housewives don't just have all the things that I really did mean to take but forgot, like clothes pegs and enough polythene bags and a can opener. They take things, which it would never have occurred to me to remember, like quilted dressing-gowns for wandering round the camp site in the early morning, and a lemon squeezer and forty-two yards of wattle fencing to surround the patch with. Frenchmen travel with their own ping-pong bats and balls, because French camping sites have the tables but no accessories, and they crease themselves up with Gallic laughter when you shamefacedly take your bottle of wine round to them because you've forgotten a corkscrew.

Any Frenchman can open any bottle, any time, with any implement. They must have to do it for their baccalaureate. The man who kept the pizza stall used to open our bottle each evening with the tip of the huge twelve-inch bladed knife that he used to flip the pizza dough over with, and it was wonderful to watch. French families don't have any problems about who's going to look after Granny and the rabbits when they're away. They all go with them. The children were delighted, on their first night abroad, to find a family of guinea pigs scuttling around in the next tent. It made them feel at home at once. Emboldened by foreign example, we took the cat with us this summer when we went camping in Scotland, but we were on a farm and everybody else had dogs and, in the middle of every night, it got out and we had to creep around in the dark under all the caravans calling "Cuddly, Cuddly". I wish our cat had a more dignified name.

When we drove into our French camping site there was a disco at the gate, full of teenagers and noise and we looked disapprovingly at each other and said the children would never get a wink of sleep. But come 10 p.m. there wasn't a sound to be heard on the site except for the raucous laughter of the English as they cracked a last bottle of wine, and the fearsome noise of the English parent disciplining his child, with slaps and whines and muffled cries of "Shut up, Sandra."

We watched a French family having a simple day out on the beach last year, grand-mère, maman, papa, le petit fils et le bébé. While maman undid a folding portable table and several chairs, grand-mère took, from a portmanteau of the kind owned by Mary Poppins, a white tablecloth, crockery, cutlery, salt, pepper and glasses (not plastic ones). Then maman heated up le bébé's bottle on a small spirit stove while le père et le petit fils blew up a portable rubber dinghy, fitted an outboard motor and took to sea. Some time later they were back with a basin full of sea urchins for lunch, which grand-mère, who had just rustled up a ratatouille on the spirit stove, proceeded to disembowel. But the French aren't even in the same league of efficiency as the Swiss or the Austrians or the Germans. It would come as no surprise to me, were a freak snowstorm suddenly to sweep the Côte d'Azur in mid-July, to see the continentals happily sitting outside their tents strapping on their skis, while the British were still rummaging around in their suitcases looking for an extra woolly. Seventy odd years of Baden-Powellism and we're hardly prepared for a thing.

49

Come to the Big Muddy

~

As the spring burgeons, and the Mickey Mouse tee-shirts appear, and the ones with Tottenham Hotspur, or Massachusetts State University, I feel a surge of quiet pride in the knowledge that I am, very likely, the only person in London and the Home Counties to own a tee-shirt with BENGOUGH, SASK. HOMECOMING '71 blazed across its chest. Almost the only person – my husband has one too. We got them for $8.50 at H. & T. Men's Wear, Main Street, Bengough, considerably reduced because the Homecoming was over. I wore mine for a while around Herne Hill until I grew over-sensitive to those strange, sideways glances, which the British give when they want to know but don't like to ask, and reverted to a blue and white striped one with no message. If you want to go and do the locum in Bengough this summer, I might lend it to you, so that you would feel at home immediately.

I daresay you're wondering what a psychiatrist was doing as a GP locum in Bengough, Sask. and it's funny you should ask. A lot of people have. He was buying a toothbrush in the chemist's across the road when a harassed-looking Indian gentleman tapped him on the shoulder and persuaded him to take over his practice for a month. He didn't seem to regard it as a problem that my husband's only experience of general practice was four weeks in Kenya, ten years ago, straight after qualifying. We could use his house, he said, and plenty of his relatives would be there, too, to take care of us. He looked as though he could use a holiday.

It's a lovely place, Bengough, and I am sure you would like it as much as we did. Luckily we brought home a booklet, which they produced as a publicity handout for their Homecoming Celebrations and Sixtieth Anniversary, so we can refresh our memories if we are ever tempted to go back again. The book has several views of the town – Main Street Bengough Looking South, at the top of the first page, with a fine view of the water tower to your right, and the quaint, corrugated-iron roofed store, and this picturesque, unmade-up road down the middle. There's a tree, too, and that's worth remarking on, because trees are not indigenous to Southern Saskatchewan, and it says a lot for the enterprise and forward-lookingness of the Bengoughians that they planted one. It looks dead in the picture, but I assure you it was alive and well last summer. Then there's a photograph of Main Street Bengough Looking North 1926, which is much the same but without the water tower and the tree and a picture of an Early Bengough Implement Dealer, and Duck Hunters at Bengough, 1921 or 22.

The prairies have their own charm – jump six inches, they say, and see 200 miles – and the citizens of Saskatchewan show a touching mixture of pride and modesty in their environment. "How do you like our country?" they ask. "We have the most wonderful sunsets." The publicity hand-out puts it like this. "The Town of Bengough is located in what is often termed the Big Muddy Area, which is located south of the town and is quite famous as the start of the Bad Lands." "Let's go down the Big Muddy," they say to each other of a Saturday night.

My husband was worried about his obstetrics, in spite of a crash revision course in the labour ward at King's one weekend. His confidence had been sapped by an experience in a mud hut in the Kenyan bush, when he thought he was delivering twins and it turned out to be just one baby and a retained placenta. We made a rough estimate of the number of deliveries he might reasonably expect in that size practice in four weeks and it was only three. He needn't have worried. We hadn't taken account of the Saskatchewan geriatric weighting factor. Large numbers of the population lived in the Senior Citizens Twilight Home. There was only one delivery, and, as that involved an arrested first stage, he despatched the woman to Regina in the air ambulance.

On the other hand, his psychiatric training came in handy, and his advanced Maudsley methods of dealing with cases like the 13-year-old lad who exposed himself three times daily in school were much admired. The boy had had treatment of course ("If you do that once more I will take this little scalpel..."), but my husband found he responded well to a less direct approach, and, after a few sessions of psychotherapy, we handed the case over to the Roman Catholic priest who was about to take a psychology course at the University of Regina.

Don't think, if you decide to take the job, that you would be heading for a social and cultural desert ("Swinging with the times," the brochure says, "in 1969 Bengough opened a library.") There was a party, too; a real North American Surprise Party such as I bet you thought only existed in the minds of American TV soap operas. It was for the butcher and his wife, who were leaving town, and it surprised them no end because they had gone out for the evening and we all had to wait for our barbecued hamburgers until they got home at 11.30. The social mores of the community are easy to follow. The men stand and drink on one side of the garden, and the women sit on chairs at the other side. You may dance with another man's wife, and tread on her toes with your cowboy boots; as the evening wears on you can even talk to her and put your Stetson on her head for a laugh, but off the dance floor no communication is apparent between the sexes.

"Sports have not been forgotten," says the Homecoming leaflet, for those that like that sort of thing, "and the town has won renown in the athletic world for its sporting activities. Also there is an entertaining golf course." There certainly is. You don't get entertainment like that at St Andrew's. What with the gopher holes and the 12-inch prairie grass on the greens, and the little wooden hut with BENG UGH G LF AND C UNTRY CLUB stencilled on its side, and the fact that none of us had handled a club before. We feel entertained even now, just thinking about it.

I expect you're surprised that a conscientious GP, entirely responsible for 74 thousand square miles of practice, could afford the time off to play golf between 6.30 and 8 p.m. every Sunday evening. Well, it seemed that somewhere over by Moose Jaw there lived a retired Scottish doctor of around 93, who was willing to stand in in an emergency. Contact was made by telephone through his housekeeper and as no one ever actually spoke to him and he was certainly never called out, we could only conclude that Putting Dr Campbell on Call was a euphemism employed by a sympathetic practice to give the hard-pressed incumbent a breather every now and then. We were offered a day out water-skiing one weekend, with the Mountie, who had got very friendly with my husband – they spent all their Saturday nights together, patching up drunken cowboys who had fallen into their own combine-harvesters. We couldn't raise Dr Campbell's housekeeper that day, but the Mountie had a radio in his car and, although it didn't reach as far as Bengough, he could remain in contact with the police station at Kayville, where we were going, so the Bengough police could get through to Kayville and Kayville could contact us and if we were in the water then they would send a car to the lake. Integration of the social services beyond the wildest dreams of Seebohm.*

Life has not always been corn and roses for Bengough. The thirties saw it "in dire straits as drought held the south in a paralysing grip. But Bengough only flinched, it did not surrender," and now, my goodness, what a character-building experience it all was because here you have it in 1972, with all of 800 people and five churches. Think of that – and you'll be able to pick and choose because all five pastors are regular surgery-goers. But wait. Don't rush precipitately off to Saskatchewan House to check that your registration will do. Let me tell you the snag. You can't drink the water. Or rather, you can, if you don't mind terracotta teeth and the taste of iron filings. But this really doesn't matter at all because Laura May, the practice secretary, has a well on her farm five miles away, with delicious water, and there are two big, red, plastic buckets with lids, in the basement, to carry it in.

I do hope somebody will go. Dr Patel must need another holiday by now and we can't manage it this year. I forgot to tell you that "Bengough is also the home of Jean Shaver who is well known for her oil paintings depicting life in the old Wild West, while an added attraction is the museum, a few miles west of Bengough, which is operated by A. Orheim and is considered by many to contain one of the finest collections in Southern Saskatchewan." You wouldn't want to miss that, would you? We didn't have time to go and I'd love to know what's in that collection. H. & T. Men's Wear might even have a few tee shirts left, too. They are probably down to a dollar by now.

In 1970 the Seebohm Committee recommended the integration of specialist areas of local authority social work to form Social Services Departments (SSDs) to bring together services for children and families and for adults.

50

Travelling hopefully

⌒

All very well for Robert Louis Stevenson to prefer travelling hopefully. Jet air travel isn't travel, for travel at least implies a sensation of passing space and time. But the Jumbo is a sensationless Tardis, suspended motionless in cloud, where the passage of time is simulated by the Pavlovian techniques of air hostesses who, like archetypal Jewish mothers, provide meals compulsively every two hours and hope that if they give you orange juice and Danish pastries at 3 am you'll believe it's morning. The only moments of excitement are provided at take-off and landing by my husband pressing his nose against the porthole and saying knowledgeably "We're not going to make it if he doesn't touch down now . . . oh, well."

Some airlines still provide travel of the real, adventurous, nineteenth century sort – small North American firms with names like Buffalo Airways, where the pilot meets you at the bottom of the steps wearing sawn-off blue jeans and a T-shirt and takes your ticket and shoves your luggage in the boot and shows you to your seat. Then he goes round the front of the plane and winds up the elastic before climbing in and driving the thing. There is no airhostess to give you so much as a barley sugar, and if you're flying over something interesting like Chappaquiddick he'll swivel round in his seat and tell you about it. "Wasn't it fun?" we said, touching down at Nantucket in a swirling sea mist after one of these trips, "So nice and casual", and then discovered they'd left our cases behind at Boston because the boot was full. "No need to worry," said the friends who met us. "That's always happening. Next plane out'll bring them. Wednesday, if the fog's lifted."

Soon one won't even be able to travel hopefully on British Rail, which now has all the accoutrements of Super-Speed – air-conditioning, automatically opening inter-compartmental doors, and the driver's voice rather self-consciously relayed into each carriage. "Good morning and welcome aboard the 10 am Inter-City London to Glasgow. We shall be leaving Euston in one minute and hope to arrive at Preston at approximately 12.32 pm. Please ask the stewards for anything you require. On behalf of British Railways I hope you enjoy your trip. Lunch will be served at 11.45 and 1 pm." Of course, if it were an aeroplane you'd have to eat them both. Coming back next day it was the beginning of the heat wave, the air-conditioning had broken down and the captain got on with driving the train and didn't say he hoped we were enjoying our trip, which was wise of him, as he might have got answered back very nastily. Just like old times though.

Very occasionally, travel can still enrich the mind. Five years or so ago I was sitting in Winnipeg airport waiting for a connection to Regina and accompanied by a small child who was exhibiting those behaviour patterns which make companies advise their senior executives to avoid important meetings while jet-lagged. The airport had long leather bench seats, facing each other in pairs, and the child and I sat at one end of the seat, driving our toy car in and out of the ashtray and wondering how to dispose of the remains of an ice-cream cone so large that neither of us could finish it. A lady in a pink suit, elderly but well preserved, stoutish around the middle but with tiny feet in patent shoes with bows on them, sat at the opposite end of the other. There were bows in her stiff white curls too, interspersed with bits of netting, and I did not know enough about the North American culture to guess whether these were to be regarded as hairdressing or millinery. I gave her a kind of sideways glance, to indicate that I was travelling hopefully and anxious to have my mind enriched by talking to the natives, but she ignored me and concentrated on her handiwork, which might have been knitting or it might have been tatting – I can't remember from this distance. I didn't blame her, because the child was not good company. After a while, another fellow traveller came and sat down opposite me, on the far end of the pink lady's bench, and he gazed up at the ceiling of the airport lounge, chewing gum. For some time the three of us sat there ignoring each other, like Englishmen in a first-class railway carriage, and then the man opposite leaned forward and, shifting the gum out of his buccal cavity into his cheek, asked me where I was going. Regina, I said. And where had I come from? London, I said. England, I added, having learnt that in that neck of the woods Ontario was the one that sprang immediately to mind. The man nodded and said he reckoned he'd maybe passed through it in '66 on his way someplace. Then I asked him where he came from himself, and he said he was on vacation from Pine Springs, Arkansas, and I said oh yes, now where was that exactly, meaning in relation to Texas and California and places like that, and he said it was kind of midway between Buckville and Cedar Glade. Pretty near Friendship, he added helpfully.

So then, to round off the conversation, I asked him where he was going, and the question obviously caused him furiously to think. He leaned back on his bench, and chewed gum a bit for inspiration, and scratched the back of his neck, and finally he leaned over towards the dame on the other end of the bench, who had gone on knitting (or tatting) her way silently through all these exchanges. "Hey, Edna," he said, "where're we going?"

51

Land of milk and honey

~

How did they manage it, those far-flung migrant World Medicine correspondents, beavering away at the end of the rainbow in the Yukon or the antipodes? How did they actually translate the routine desire to emigrate, which springs up every time the bank statement comes in, into such get up and go, decisive action? Didn't they, too, have a Greek chorus of friends like ours starting up every time we try to do it, telling us that it is all due to the male menopause, this desire to up sticks and tackle a new environment, talking about cultural starvation and the quality of life, by which they mean that being able to watch *The Goodies* on television makes up for not being able to afford tickets for Covent Garden? Were they not asked how they could contemplate living anywhere but London, in the chauvinist way of Londoners to whom Bolton and Brisbane are equally beyond the pale? Were they not halted in their tracks at each attempted sortie across the Atlantic by cries of "You'll never stand the climate"?

You have to keep trying, though; it keeps the spirits up and the bank manager quiescent with idle promises – this

235

summer we even got as far as testing the cold water of foreign parts with a tentative, exploratory toe. Winnipeg, the Croydon of the prairies, was not, in early summer, as bad as we had been led to expect. True, the prospective immigrant is easy to please, falling on each reassuring similarity with home in gratified amazement. "Oh look," we said to each other, "they've got lilac, they've got honeysuckle, they've got Marks & Spencer," eager to believe the best of the place, like castaways finding mutton bones in suspected cannibal territory.

You don't need to worry about the winter, all the Canadians told us – and they love to tell you too, because they are obsessed with their weather far and away beyond any English obsession. They have a whole radio channel devoted just to regional temperatures and weather forecasts and sports reports, alternating throughout the day. Everybody likes the winter, they said, the little kids look forward to the winter, although of course when there's a blizzard they have to walk backwards to school. Or backwards home again, depending. Anyway, it's sunny and there aren't that many blizzards. The trouble is just that the snow never goes; that what falls in October is still around in April, though grubbier. One month they've never had a frost in – July, was it? Or August? Nobody could remember but everyone agreed there is one absolutely reliable, high summer, frost-free month. If only they could remember which.

They ski in Manitoba in the winter: not down hills; there are no hills in Manitoba. But there are rivers and the rivers freeze and everyone puts on strange, narrow little skis, which hang on the wall of every home we visited, and they walk up and down the rivers on these skis. The corner of Portage and Main Street, by the British Airways ticket office, is a source of pride to Winnipeggers. It is said to be the coldest, windiest place in North America. On the way to confirm our reservations home, I struggled against the wind, funnelled down Main Street after a thousand mile journey across the prairie, and needed no convincing. I asked the man at the ticket office if it was always like this. "Yes, ma'am," he said, beaming with pride. "Except in summer. Summer, it's the hottest and windiest." July, that would be. Or August.

There is plenty to do in Winnipeg, besides walking around on skis. There is the Ballet and the Opera and the Symphony. They figured largely in a publicity handout on Saskatchewan and Manitoba, which we had read in the aeroplane coming over. Poor Saskatchewan had been pretty much glossed over in the face of Manitoba's greater cultural temptations. "When in Saskatchewan," the brochure had said, "do not fail to visit the open-cast coal mine at Estevan." We had dinner with a doctor and his wife who told us about a couple, newly arrived in Winnipeg last winter, who joined everything, went to everything and then found they hadn't a Saturday free, not one, the whole winter. "How about Wednesday?" said my husband obstructively. "What if they'd wanted to do something on a Wednesday?" "Wednesdays," said our hosts thoughtfully, "well Wednesdays might present a problem." June presented a bit of a problem too. The girl at the ticket office at the Hudson Bay Company store had no tickets for the Opera or the Ballet or the Symphony because the season hadn't started. September through April, she said, that was the season. Any time I wanted a ticket, September through April, she'd be happy to get me one.

The sex shops aren't up to Soho. Or rather, I don't think they can be but I cannot do a quality comparison because in London I give them only a swift sideways glance in case anyone I know sees me and thinks I am compensating. In Winnipeg, secure in brazen anonymity, I pressed my nose against the window and found it just another of life's let downs. No dildos; no vibrators, no whips or chains or natty gents' rubber suitings; just some rather tepid-looking underwear, a pair of satin sheets and a bawd game.

The bookshop next to the sex shop didn't have the range of Foyle's, but the service was keener. ("I couldn't find it," I heard one Foyle's salesgirl tell another the other day, "so I told her we hadn't got it". There's a girl brimming over with job satisfaction.) The window featured a display of the works of Winnipeg's author of the month, a lady born of the union of Patience Strong with William McGonagall, whose specially illustrated inspirational verses were inscribed on pale blue satin framed in gilt-edged plastic. But the people we met were as nice as the ones back home, and the meals they gave us as good as any we have over here, and the only film we wanted to see was on at the cinema, but we were so overloaded with hospitality that we didn't have time to see it.

The friends for whom your potential emigration is vicarious experience are as irritating as the ones strewing doubts along your path. "How lucky you are," they say, sitting back replete and immovable after dinner; what an experience. "Wish it was me," they say, then hurriedly, in case the fates overhear and intervene, "but too many commitments, too busy, too old, too many children, but my goodness how I envy you, what an opportunity, you'd be mad to miss it".

Opportunities are nice, of course, but unpredictable. I keep thinking of a friend of ours, a musician, who tells the story of how, on tour in America, he found himself after a concert at an elegant party on board somebody's sumptuous yacht, looking out over starlit water, an elderly American lady at his side telling him all about how her husband, in his youth, had wanted to be a musician – could have been a musician – only his father had insisted on his going into the family business. "It's just terrible," she had said, "the way parents blight their children's lives. I tell you, his Daddy simply ruined that boy's opportunities." And our friend nodded his agreement in a hazy alcoholic way and just then a steward appeared at the lady's elbow. "Mrs Rothschild," he said, "you're wanted on the telephone."

52

Holistic get-together

1iere anglais: Two tickets to downtown Montreal, please.
Conducteur de l'autobus: Quoi?
2ieme anglaise: Il ne comprend pas. Il faut que tu parle français.

1iere anglais: Il comprend parfaitement s'il te plait. Il est seulement totallement bolshie. '

2ieme anglaise: Quand en Rome, faire comme les Romans.

1iere anglais: Certainement, mais ce n'est pas Rome. Ce n'est pas Paris either. C'est le British Commonwealth et je refuse de pander a ce Nationalisme ridiculeux.

2ieme anglaise: Et moi, je refuse de rester chez Montreal airport toute la nuit parceque tu refuse de parler français au point du principle. Deux billets a downtown Montreal SVP.

Conducteur de l'autobus: Two tickets to downtown Montreal? Certainly, madam.

And when you do speak French they pretend they can't understand your accent. "Ou est la riviere St Lawrence?" I asked a taxi-driver our first evening in the place, making polite conversation, trying to put him at his ease. I thought

239

he made heavy weather of the question till I discovered next day that Montreal is on an island, entirely surrounded by the St Lawrence. Did you know that? I didn't. So it may have been geographical confusion rather than simple non-communication.

But Quebec is the only part of North America where non-communication has ever been a problem. Usually it's more a matter of dealing with the problems of over-communication. The second half of this trip was a conference in Toronto about clean living and holistic (there's a word someone ought to suppress) health. It was one of those very American-style events where the first thing the chairman does is to tell the audience to stand up and relate to each other, get acquainted, shake hands with their neighbours, spread a little warmth and love and brotherhood around. When this happens I go rigid and my toes curl under and my stomach drops a few inches: It's' not that I don't think that warmth and love and brotherhood are fine things. It is just that I am too British to be able to achieve them in, well, let's be conservative and say under about a couple of hours. And in the New World, brother, that's too long, too long.

How can I put myself in a nutshell for my neighbour in the time it takes to give a warm handclasp and a forced grin? And vice versa? A girl in the row in front showed how it was done. "Hi, I'm Beth," she said, striding up and down the row grasping every proffered hand and reaching for the ones that weren't, "and I'm a computer programs analyser and I think the idea of the holistic family is our only real hope for the future which is why this conference is so terribly important and why I am so glad to be here today". She was a beautiful girl and she exuded the confidence that they all absorb with their peanut butter and jelly sandwiches. She also had the right sort of name. Mine is too dignified somehow, too regal in its associations for such gross informality. Simple rules govern North American names, designed to deal with this need for immediate intimacy.

1. No name shall have more than one syllable.
2. Any name with one syllable shall be made disyllabic.
3. Any name with two syllables shall be curtailed.
4. Thus Joan and Charles become Joanie and Charlie and you can work out for yourselves what happens to Susan and David.
5. Nobody seems to be called things like Franklin D. Roosevelt any more.

The closing ceremony was even worse. My husband was quick enough to spot it coming and left the hall at a speed too fast for the human eye to follow, except mine, but, by the time I'd realised why he'd chickened out, it was too late and I was flattened against the wall with the Gestalt therapists and the chiropractors and the psychic healers and the chap who did hair analysis and about 300 other warm loving people, forming a vast hand-clasping ring, gently swaying to the rhythm of a moving song played by a grossly overweight guitar player.

The only comfort was that the elderly gentleman, whose left hand I was forced to hold in my own reluctant right, obviously had hang-ups similar to mine. We both stared at our feet and directed neutral feelings into our joined hands and I felt less alone. Then I felt a tug on my left hand and noticed that my other neighbour, a lady somewhat shorter than me, was standing on tiptoe, attempting to kiss my cheek. So I stooped a little so she could reach and then, because I'm not that churlish and it seemed only courteous, I kissed her back. "No, no," she hissed, "pass it on". The elderly gentleman and I got the message at the same time and he quickly turned his head so that all I could get at was a spot somewhere behind his left ear. At that he crumbled altogether and shot out of the door, to be dogged, no doubt, by the misfortunes that commonly attend the breakers of chain letters. However, the whole incident may well have a profitable outcome. The lady clasping my left hand, the one with the wart on it, turned out to be a faith healer. I am almost sure the wart has shrunk a little since Sunday. I'll let you know how it goes along.

AND FINALLY

~

2020 seemed like a good time to gather all the pieces in this book together, review one's past, or at any rate a chunk of it – after all, no one seems quite sure how much future any of us are going to have. What an extraordinary year it's been. We left London over a year ago, on March 10th 2020, herded up to our holiday house in the Highlands to join the sheep by the family, who felt we'd be more out of harm's way here. Just for a couple of weeks we thought, till they get the virus under control, and came up with the cat, a suitcase and the clothes we stood up in. A lesson in what one actually needs to survive! So restful never to have to think what shall I wear when the choice is only either an extra sweater or a clean one. Neither of us has had a haircut since we arrived – who needs that when you have a perfectly good pair of scissors?

And who needs to spend an hour pushing a trolley round a supermarket when Tesco can give us a food delivery about once a fortnight, we have wonderful neighbours who would never let us starve, and most mornings we drive to our local (stretching the term a bit, it's 8 miles away) village shop where we get the paper and milk and more or less anything else we've run out of. To be honest, if we're thinking about Quality of Life, day-to-day survival is a lot harder back in Herne Hill. The other day, when my husband tried to back the car out and got stuck in a snowdrift, our farmer friend Brian came right over with his tractor and dragged him out. Just then the Tesco van arrived and got stuck in the same snowdrift so Brian pulled him out too. You'd never get that sort of service from the AA.

We have been coming up here for summer visits more or less every year since my mother-in-law bought the house in 1960. Not actually to *live* in of course – in those days it had no mains electricity, no mains water supply, just a 2kw generator and a tank on the hill – and certainly not to live in in winter. She would come over in June and belt back to her home in Kenya at the beginning of September. Since 1987, when every house along our three-mile stretch of road was finally connected to the mains, we have often managed a brief Christmas visit, too, but always scuttled back to Herne Hill when the snow fell and the going got rough.

At first I thought Life in Lockdown was going to be rather like what I thought retirement would be like but never was: plenty to read (the main advantage of old age is that you're never short of something to read because you can't remember the books you've already read even when you're half way through them); and a few projects (like this one) we've been putting off for months because there was no time to do them. But of course now, almost a year later, everyone has adjusted and life is more or less back to what it used to be like but a lot easier in some ways. One day last week, for example, my husband had to give a paper at a conference in San Francisco at 4.0 p.m. and then race back to London for a Committee meeting at 5.30 and be home for supper at 8.0. You couldn't have done that back in the Olden Days. And you don't even have to cope with jet lag. I'd be willing to bet that this sort of thing will continue even when life gets back to normal. Zooming has become a way of life and communication.

One of the problems of lockdown life is that the days have no markers. Thursday is Bin Day but there is absolutely nothing else to distinguish it from Monday, Tuesday, Wednesday or Friday. Saturday is ok. Or rather it's ok if we have been able to collect our newspaper because on Saturdays we are able to get *The Guardian*. *The Guardian* doesn't seem to penetrate the farthest reaches of Scotland, except (don't ask me why) on Saturdays. Monday to Friday we have to make do with *The Times*. However, in so many ways, lockdown has turned the whole concept of second best, making do, etc., etc., on its head. It's rather like Heinz Tomato Soup. Twelve months ago, so far as I was concerned, Heinz tomato soup was a last resort lunch, something you might give the children if you were in a hurry while you nibbled a quick digestive biscuit and cheese yourself. How wrong I was. Heinz tomato soup is delicious and why I ever thought otherwise I shall never understand. Anyway, back to *The Times*. *The Times* has *two* codewords every day. *The Guardian* has one a day and **NONE** on Saturdays. For nearly a year I have tried not to let this affect my deep down basic loyalty to *The Guardian*, but it did come under severe pressure every Saturday. And then, miraculously, on Saturday February 20th, 2021 one of life's dreams came true: a Codeword! In *The Guardian*! I shall chalk it up, along with the tomato soup, as yet another positive by-product of lockdown.

In case you are wondering how we spend the free time that occasionally comes our way, I'll pass on to you the leisure activities that we have found irreplaceable, in case you ever find yourselves in isolation in the middle of a Scottish moor in winter.

1. Pheasant bets. Every morning before breakfast, when we set off for Inverarnie for the newspaper, we each place a bet on the number of pheasants we will see on the journey there. In fact we intend to write a useful scientific paper on this,

correlating the number seen with the wind speed/ambient temperature/rainfall/ sunshine. So far no correlations have been found. Road kill do not count.

2. Log-jam Jengo. This is a version of the well-known children's game, which involves removing a brick from a tower without bringing the whole lot down: played in the garage where logs are stacked floor to ceiling, and my part of the game is to fill the bags with logs so my husband can carry them in. Not suitable for small children, and players over the age of 80 are allowed to use a walking stick to undo a log jam at a safe(r) distance.

And, if we've really got nothing else to do, we can just look out of the window and watch the weather and the wildlife. It's the wildlife, which is really fascinating. Whether we have more time to observe it, or whether the lack of people and cars means there's more of it about, I don't know. We've watched a roe deer being chased across a field by a hare until the deer finally gave up and jumped over a fence, and a pheasant sitting in the middle of a field being dive-bombed repeatedly by another bird. Red squirrels and curlews and so many birds I don't know – I must get one of those apps, which help you to identify them. This year is the first we have seen all four seasons come and go, watched the short life of the lambs from birth to market, and the vast flock of wild geese, whose offspring we watched grow from fluffy balls to goslings, who always crossed the road in front of us when we drove to get the paper, escorted by the pair of adult geese that we assumed were the parents, to youngsters old enough to set off with the flock to – who knows where? But I hope they'll be back this year.